The Easy Guide to Online Marketing

Published by
The Bourquin Group
1135 Terminal Way #106
Reno, NV 89502
www.bourquingroup.com

Note to readers:

Acknowledgements:

As with all books, this one didn't write itself, nor did I write it alone. It is really a compilation of the questions and complaints I received from potential clients and actual clients. Most of them were related to Facebook, and now that Google has Launched Google+, 95% of the information applies. Included in this book is the step by step guide from *How to Market On Facebook For Free*.

Each time a problem or question came up I made a note. The list got pretty long and with the help of a couple of business owners who acted as a test case.

When Google Launched Google+, we used the same rules to build pages for several clients and tested all of the same rules that we learned on Facebook. There are very few differences, and I tried to highlight them the best I could within this book.

Many of our clients were test cases for learning what the other companies were doing wrong and what the big search engines really looked for.

Thank you to all of our clients and we look forward to many more years of growth for you.

Introduction

When I started my first business everyone who called wanted money from me. Yellow Pages, White Pages, Internet Ads, Golf Course Bench ads and the list went on!

The worst part is that I had no idea about advertising or marketing. My first customers were friends, family and dumb luck.

So what did I do? At first I started buying ads every where until I ran out of money. Then I learned how to buy different phone numbers for each ad for $200 per line per month so I could see which ads worked.

When I ran out of money again, the internet only had a few thousand domain names in use. It was the wild west of marketing.

Today there are millions of domain names and you can get VoIP forwarding numbers for a couple of dollars a month.

So how do you keep from getting lost in the sea of businesses online?

That's what this book is for. After building several companies and learning more about marketing than I ever wanted, I started a marketing company. Not just any marketing company, a marketing company that works for small business.

This book really should be "The Easy Guide To Internet Marketing 2nd Edition" but, we decided there is more to it than the internet itself.

If You opened this book thinking internet marketing doesn't work, those guys are just "lucky", then let me show you how to "get lucky" with online and internet marketing.

Just about every Business Owner knows that there is a better way to reach customers. Most of the time they just feel like they are too busy or it costs too much money. Many say "The internet doesn't work." knowing deep down it does, they just haven't found "*the secret*".

Just like all those guys calling about phone book ads and billboards, there are hoards of people out there bombarding you with phone calls, email's and junk mail trying to get money from you to "be number one on Google".

Have you built a website only to be disappointed but don't know why? We have replaced $50,000 websites, with simple effective $3,000 websites that owners can update on their own, and those sites bring in the customers the $50,000 sites where chasing away.

In this book, I'll show you why and how to fix those big glaring problems you are probably seeing without knowing it. Have you tried Social Marketing and just found it to be a huge waste of time? We'll fix that too. Do your pay per click or PPC ads bring in nothing but bills?

You are right that Internet Marketing done the wrong way is a huge waste of time and money. I see it happening every time I am introduced to a new customer. You are not alone.

If you have been frustrated by Internet Marketing, Social Marketing or whatever you want to call it, you are among the group that most business owners find themselves in and I want to help you fix that. I also know you might not be able to afford my services, so I wrote this book to give every small business owner a chance.

You need to worry about your business, not Internet Marketing. That said, there is a way to build your business using Internet Marketing and Social Media that is cost effective and won't take up all of your time.

With this book, I will help you build a simple and effective online marketing program that includes social media like Facebook, Yelp! and Manta. This program can all be done for free, and it can be done by you. You can also build a simple guide and hire someone if that is what you want to do. I'll also show you how to get it done at a very fair price using contractors online or hiring it out the right way.

The other area I see money wasted is print marketing. Before you finish this book, I am going to share with you how to use everything you learn here about internet marketing to boost your print marketing returns too! Call it a free bonus.

Using Internet, Social and Information Marketing, a select few business owners really connect. Combined this is "Online Marketing". With small budgets and very little effort, they keep customers coming in the doors, and coming back for more. I have seen it in all kinds of businesses. No matter what kind of business you have, the right approach can pay off.

I want you to be one of those select business owners who know how to leverage the power of the Internet. I want to help you build a stronger business and a better connection to your clients. With the *Easy Guide to Online Marketing*, I am going to help you create an online presence for your business, and teach you how to do it for next to nothing.

Originally titled the **Easy Guide To Social Marketing**, we realized that many people weren't using the term Social Marketing correctly when they were looking for answers online. Free research like we did for this book is one of the best tools you as a business owner can have in your toolbox, and we are going to show you how to do it.

The Easy Guide to Social Marketing will be out soon, it will just be different than this book. It will be for companies without a website. A book for very small startups and home businesses.

This book is the culmination of several years of work, research and observation from the inside of the online marketing and Internet Presence business. Included in this book is all of the key information from *"How to Market on Facebook For Free"* also.

I want to help you learn simple techniques to observe, participate and engage in social media that help your business. Every business owner and manager knows they need to have an Internet Presence, and market online, but most don't have a plan, and are overwhelmed trying to figure out all of the different websites. After all with 100,000 new websites hitting the internet every hour, how do you know where to go?

If you have been feeling frustrated with online advertising, your website and more specifically social media, you are not alone.

Business owners from all over the country talk to us regularly to learn how they can improve all of these areas without breaking the bank or spending hundreds of hours glued to their computer.

Your problem isn't as unique as you think. Lots of business owners and managers are feeling the same frustration you have probably felt. The point of this book is to make it simple and easy for you to help your business succeed using tools that are out there waiting for you.

You might not have had any idea where to start and now you are holding the blueprints for creating a simple and easy to execute plan that is proven to work over and over.

Social media is arguably the most important and most cost effective marketing tool available to a business today, and yet GM pulled out of its $10 Million Dollar a year Facebook program just as Facebook went public. The cancellation of GM's Facebook Marketing program led many small business owners and business writers to wonder if Social Media really has any value.

Social Media can be the most expensive and time consuming channel in your marketing program if it isn't being used effectively. Clearly a decision maker at GM didn't feel it was money being well spent. Let's keep it simple and not try to over analyze things.

While talking with hundreds of business owners and marketing managers it became clear that social media was the biggest challenge facing them today. Most felt totally out of control as fans, competitors and even black hat marketing companies posted information on their social media site.

A couple of issues kept filtering themselves to the top, and the result was always the same. In one direction the business found success without breaking the bank or spending all day locked in a room looking at social media sites, and in the other direction were businesses like GM that just threw in the towel and pushed out of social media as far as they could while they regroup.

I doubt that GM has given up on social media as a marketing tool, I think they just became frustrated with results that are difficult to measure. I am sure financial analysts are popping antacids and staring at numbers that appear to have no cause and effect while deciding if their social media program works.

Admittedly, if not done right, Social Marketing can be very hard to measure. If you don't build loyalty very quickly it can be a losing game. Sites like livingsocial.com or groupon.com offer potential new customers a great deal, that usually costs you money, and lots of it. The idea is that you will get these new clients to stick. The reality is that they rarely do. They will go to the next deal faster than you can say "Hey, where is my money?"

If any executives at GM read this and agree, I would be glad to get their observations directly

I. Purpose

Like a business, every book in the business category should have a specific purpose. This one does. Simply stated, **With this book I want to give you a solid foundation and understanding of marketing your business or service online without the fluff that wastes your time**.

Included are simple yet effective methods to leverage your website, Social Media and your clients to connect them and create better communications which lead to better business. This book isn't going to be all inclusive. What you are getting are the tools and essential components you need to use online marketing to build your business.

In some areas you may already know what you need to know. That is why I set each header in bold. If you know the difference between a **Facebook Profile** and a **Facebook Page**, you can skip that sections where you see that in bold and save more time. Isn't getting more time for yourself the reason you started a business in the first place?

For instance, in this book I will cover podcasting very briefly. Podcasting isn't required and is a completely different tool in the online marketing arsenal. If after reading the chapter on podcasting you decide you are ready to podcast, we have an *Easy Guide To Podcasting* available at *EasyGuideBooks.com*

I did this to keep the cost of each book down and to let you decide exactly what parts you wanted to know more about.

This is the starting gate.

There is also another theme that is carried throughout the book that is one of the most powerful secrets to success in business. Don't worry, if you read the entire book, I will tell you the secret more than once. If you need help with it, I have an online coaching program.

The social aspect of business and the Internet changes everything. You aren't asking for sales, you are asking for referrals. You aren't posting specials, you are directing and controlling influence, while building (or destroying) credibility. Posting a 10% off or even a 50% off coupon on Facebook won't do you any good if the same coupon is sitting at the store all day or is in the mailbox.

There is a major retailer that allows employees to hide coupons behind the counter so that anyone who asks can get the better price. Eventually two things happen. First no one pays attention to the social deal, and second they no longer even think of it as a deal, getting a discount becomes an expectation. This is the real danger of Social Marketing and how you destroy credibility.

The auto industry is another example where we can see misguided marketing. Many big brands dug themselves into a deep hole with rebates and cheap financing. When you do that too long, the customers expect the discounts and getting back to normal pricing can be very challenging and expensive..

One of the most powerful techniques in marketing is the *power of limited supply*. Limited supply taps our social need to belong. In marketing there are four main social needs, belonging, fear of loss, need to learn, and status shift. Limited supply is one of the few selling methods that touches all four of these psychological triggers.

Belonging is most affected by rules of "limited supply". We all want to be in the group that everyone wants to be in. Belonging is a very powerful social need for humans, and no one wants to be left out.

The key to using limited supply is to create something that is genuinely "limited" and not reappearing every Friday, or "limited editions" like Toyota that are simply an upgraded model that is available every day.

While the initial boost in sales is both addicting it is also dangerous like a drug that becomes less effective with each use until it kills you from overdose.

The best internet marketers and brick and mortar stores use the power of limited supply to great success. Have you ever been to Costco to buy something you saw last week only to find they don't carry it anymore? I bet you won't make that mistake again. Seasonal flavors like Egg Nog show up at lots of places for a limited time.

JCP aka JC Penny is rebuilding under a new CEO using the same rules that built several great companies in the 1930's. Many of those companies which still follow those rules are doing well today.

Building credibility and social influence can be a powerful online marketing tool. It also takes time, patience and a solid understanding of what your customers really want. If you abuse your influence you can very quickly lose both your credibility and your influence leaving you with nothing to show for your efforts.

This book is intended to also help you decide whether you should hire a Social Marketing company like mine, the *Bourquin Group*, or do the work internally. Quite frankly, the work will always be better and more cost effective internally if you follow the rules in this book.

Why? The simple answer is nobody knows your real customers and employees better than you. When you hire someone to do this for you, they need to spend time getting an understanding of your business, and scour information to get that same understanding if they are going to do a decent job for you. One way or another you are going to pay for that time. When you hire a Social Marketing company, part of that work is in the setup fees, the rest is amortized out over the next few months.

In some rare cases, I really know both the client and their customer. In Southern California I am in *TruSpeed* every month, sometimes every week. I know all of the employees, and have met several customers. When I go skiing or hiking in the Tahoe area, I stop into Cake Tahoe pretty regularly as well. The other clients I attend to personally take several hours of research and usually a phone call or two a month so that I can stay connected to what is happening in their business. That time costs money.

By the time you finish this book, your business should have a clearly defined customer, and a clearly defined destination and you will be able to clearly define a path for your Internet and Social Marketing that connects the two.

I like to think of that path that connects your customers to your business destination like a flight path of an airplane. It is more direct than a train, bus or a car. In fact a flight path is much more direct than any other path I know of. Even a direct flight path needs direction and a destination, and that is why you are here.

Just like a car on the road stuck in traffic or a jet liner headed straight for a thunderstorm, you also need to recognize dangers and unnecessary delays along your path.

II. Scope

Understanding the scope and reach of social media is critical to any online marketing program. Very soon you will know what you can and can't do with Social Marketing and how to do it. You will be familiar with the major players, and how you can use them to shorten the path between you and your customers.

In order to help you get familiar with the big players in Social Marketing and the second level niche players, I am going to give a brief introduction to each of the sites we consider critical today, and introduce a couple that might become heavy hitters.

After each website or social media site is introduced, I'll cover what kinds of businesses should be using this site and how. I'll also discuss how to advertise on those sites if you choose to do it.

Most **money** spent on social media sites isn't Social Marketing. It is about positioning. You are trying to get your ad or information in front of a potential client who is looking at a competitor. It is more like fighting for a client then actually connecting with them. That is why so much money is wasted.

Conversion rates are very low on most social media sites, and over time I expect that the churn will slow down and those sites could be in trouble.

You might be asking "If the ads don't work, why do people pay for them?". That is a simple two part answer:

1. The people paying don't measure the results, so they don't know they are wasting money until it is too late, or
2. As soon as they are sure of the lack of results they stop advertising.

When your competitor stops advertising, that is when your phone rings with a salesman on the other end because "A great spot just opened up!"

Unlike the How To Market On Facebook (or Google+) For Free books, this book will not have step by step directions for every website. Since Facebook is significantly different, the steps from "How To Market On Facebook For Free" are included in the Facebook section. The rest will only be guidelines on how to set up the account.

Most accounts are very easy once you get on the site. The real issue for most people trying to run a business is even knowing that another site exists because there are so many.

Trying to create a step by step guide for every site would be huge. If you need more personalized help, we have consulting services available. They really aren't that hard once you complete the worksheets in this book.

One thing I do suggest is that you create a separate email and password for all of your social media work and create a list of all of the social sites you created an account on. It is easy to forget these things when you are trying to run a business. Doing something like YourName@gmail.com makes it much easier and doesn't clutter up your inbox with all of the spammy offers you are sure to receive for getting into the Social Media Market.

For the purposes of this book, I will use "owners" to mean "owners", "managers" or "leaders".

III The Top Business Mistake

Every business started for a reason. The longer you have been in business the more likely you are to have forgotten why. If you haven't started a business yet, this chapter alone could be your lifesaver.

The secret formula to a successful business is a two step formula. You can't have one part without the other. Some businesses have neither. Without both the business will eventually go away.

Sadly, more often than not when I am brought into a business that is either in trouble or on the verge of big trouble, I can see this problem within 30 minutes of walking in the door. If I can't get an agreement to correct the problem within an hour, I leave, don't charge and move on to the next client.

My belief in this issue is so strong, I will not take a client who can't fill in the blanks of the formula for success.

The Secret Formula Part I:

So what is the formula? The first part is a problem statement. What problem are you solving for your customer and how big is that potential market?

That question alone will cause a lot of business owners to stumble, and before you go any further, I suggest you answer it and write it down. If you have a chisel and tablet, then hammer away and hang it on the wall so you remember what you do every day.

The mistake that many small business owners make when starting a business is they don't solve problems for other people, they solve problems for themselves.

If you started your business because you thought the company you worked for charged to much and you could do it cheaper you have started up a very slippery slope. It can be done but it is very hard, and that is generally your problem if your old boss is making money. The other customers obviously felt the price was high, but not high enough to go elsewhere.

Don't make price personal, and don't take it personally if a few people think your price is too high.

Sometimes people love a hobby so much a friend will say "you should open a store" or something like that and they do. Again they solved a problem for themselves, but it doesn't mean they can build a viable business.

Make sure you are solving a problem a lot of people have, and that you can solve it at a very nice profit.

The Secret Formula Part II:

The second area to fill in in the formula is about purpose. The companies that are normally in the most trouble have the same answer in both sections "cheaper". Cheaper isn't a solution and it isn't a purpose. Even Wal-Mart gets that.

The Wal-Mart slogan says it all. "Save Money, Live Better". The slogan doesn't say "cheaper". Sam Walton found a way to make "cheaper" have a purpose.

Purpose is what allows you to leave your business in the hands of others and allows you to hire better.

How?

Purpose gives employees a reason to be there other than money for time. Nobody really wants to trade money for time. Most people do simply because they are handcuffed by society to their lifestyle. Rent, car payments, credit cards, eating out all add up to a need for money.

Most people only know how to get a job that pays them by the time put in. Even most sales people book their sales based on a monthly need. No one has taught them how to earn based on performance or value.

Success Tip :

There is a third less common mistake many new business owners make. That is thinking they want to serve wealthy clients and charge a lot for each client. There is a saying "Serve the Classes, Live With The Masses."

There are some businesses that are very successful serving the upper class, but they are also very high cost businesses that took decades to build. Unless you have a billion in the bank, find a solution for a problem that a lot of people have, and make a few cents off of each person.

Most companies that make a lot of money serve a lot of people, Google can make just a penny a click and reap billions a year, Apple products look expensive and yet there is a line out the door every time there is a new model, and all of those people don't have Black AMEX cards in their pocket. Apple doesn't serve everyone, but they don't cater to the elite either. There is a peak profit/ demand for every product.

When Steve Jobs turned the reigns of Apple over to Gil Amelio, the purpose changed. It was a subtle difference that the culture couldn't handle. With Steve Jobs gone it will be interesting to see if Tim Cook has the right purpose in his leadership for Apple to continue.

In an earlier version of this book I mentioned Ford. The CEO had come from Boeing and he was the right guy at the right time for Ford. Since then Ford has become profitable without declaring bankruptcy, and the CEO has moved on. Now the question is, can the new CEO carry the purpose.

Now you might be asking, how can a burger shop or a pizza place or even a cup cake store have a purpose. The answer is that the successful ones do.

If you want your business to grow and succeed you need a purpose. Something your employees and fans can grab onto and run with.

Without an easy to understand purpose for your business that your fans and employees can run with, you are the only one that will be doing the running.

Mel Abraham in his book **The Entrepreneurs Solution** discusses the importance of purpose as the meaning your business has to you that it can also have to your employee's and your customers.

If your business purpose doesn't mean anything to you employees, it won't mean anything to your customers. Over time you are a commodity at best, out of business at worst.

It is when you, your employees and customers all share the same purpose that you achieve the greatest success.

IV. Definitions and Players

This list isn't in alphabetical order, so bear with me. I put it in something closer to the order of importance as a business owner relates to the term.

As you go through the definitions, don't feel like you need to memorize them all, or any of them for that matter. This section is more of a reference point more than anything else. The sections later will give you a step by step guide and a checklist to help you keep your sanity, and keep from giving your life to the computer.

As a business owner, you have a lot of choices to make. The first one is whether or not you are going to be a business owner, or create a job for yourself where you happen to own the business.

If you own an auto shop and work on cars all day, that is your job. If you own a shop and hire mechanics to do the work, that is a business. Social Media can be contracted out at varying levels depending on your needs.

You can also have a receptionist or office staff do a lot of this as long as you do the most important step, which is to follow up. You need to know that what is being presented online matches what is happening in your business. These definitions should help you understand what is happening online regardless of who is doing it, you, your staff, your contractor or your customers.

Social Media - Online interactive multi-faceted websites are being lumped into the generic box labeled Social Media. Yelp! and Foursquare are very different from MySpace or Google+, yet many people consider them all social media.

We call it social media because the person or business that is the point of focus isn't in charge of the message. This is where many business owners are confused, worried, stressed out and concerned. A long list of one star ratings on Yelp! can be very damaging to a restaurant whether they earned them or not.

Many of the creators of Social Media Sites like Mark Zuckerberg of Facebook see themselves as the champions of democracy and truth. That is clearly changing now that Facebook has investors. Google on the other hand has no such direction. Google is just trying to stay relevant, and given their size, you can't ignore it as a business owner.

Social Media relies on transparency, and yet you can still tweak the system a little. For instance, you can't say you were at Cake Tahoe, and brag about how great the cupcakes were unless your phone is close enough to check in.

When the owner of Cake Tahoe posts that she has the best cupcakes in town, what happens? People are more than happy to post their opinion to stroke their own ego, so when Cake Tahoe delivers the greatest cupcake ever, the patrons become fans and tell their friends. If a business doesn't deliver, they *still tell their friends.*

Where the tweaking comes in is reviews. You don't have to set foot in a business to create a review, and that is where the danger lies. Trying to defend a false review is worse than leaving it alone. Eventually it gets filtered if it is false. There are people who will try and cheat no matter what.

On rare occasion we have protested and won when a competitor badmouthed our client. The problem came later when the site started filtering out the 5 star reviews also. If we just let the one bad fake review sit there, the 20 five star reviews would have crowded it out.

Often when owners call us, they begin with the position that the one star rating is a "difficult" customer. Nine out of ten times when we reach the customer, it turns out something did go horribly wrong. A quick call from the owner, a free cup of coffee and everything can be fixed.

Many business owners think they don't control the message and that is what worries them about Social Media. The truth is the business 99% controls the message by its actions and delivery. If you say you have the best cupcakes and they are, you win. If you say you have the lowest happy hour beer prices in town and you don't, you lose.

Social Media can be an integrity check for your business. It is also the world's best feedback and survey tool. If you want to know how your customers like the live music on Wednesdays at your pizza place, all you have to do is check your receipts and read the comments on Facebook, Google+, Yelp! and Foursquare. You don't need to pay for expensive surveys to know what is happening in your business.

Social Media Marketing - Many times just called Social Marketing, Social Media Marketing is the active attempt to directly engage existing customers using social media sites such as Facebook, Yelp!, Google Plus and Foursquare. The purpose is simply to bring those existing customers back and turn them into your invisible sales force. Keep this in mind every time you post or tweet. Start by asking "Would I share this?" or "Would my friends send this to me?"

My favorite use of real time marketing is the restaurant manager that tweets out deals whenever the place is slow. His regulars are a small percentage of the people who come in, the rest are their friends.

Facebook® - Facebook is just one of thousands of social media sites around the world. The problem they face as a business is size. More people are members of Facebook than live in several countries. As Facebook adds features to try and hold off smaller sites like Yelp! and Angies List, they get more complicated and alienate some users.

As a business owner this is a challenge because there is so much happening, you can get distracted by the noise and forget why you are spending any time with Facebook in the first place. I believe that is what happened to GM and why they pulled $10 Million in advertising money from Facebook. It wasn't that Facebook doesn't work, it was that GM forgot why they were there and what they were using it for. When GM lost direction, Facebook didn't work for them.

Facebook in my mind is still the single most underutilized tool in every businesses marketing arsenal. Mine included. And no, I don't work for Facebook, and Facebook didn't pay me to say that.

If I talk about me, Scott Bourquin, as an author, there are more ways to connect and spread my message on Facebook than any other platform except a website. The difference is, Facebook will help me spread my message if it is one that resonates with a community.

A website might never get found if I don't put a lot of effort into it. Our company offers SEO and SEM services and I can tell you for any starting business, start with free Facebook services, and then look at your own website.

For a company like GM, their problem is the breadth of interest in GM products. There are fans for the Volt, fans for the Corvette, and even a few who are fans of both. There are Sierra guys and Camaro girls, and Sierra girls and Camaro guys.

Approaching all of these different micro markets is a challenge for every big company. GM can't approach Facebook as GM any more than Procter and Gamble can approach it as Proctor and Gamble. GM needs to approach Facebook fans as Corvette fans and Trucks fans and Proctor and Gamble needs to see Detergent fans and Shampoo fans.

Just because a customer loves Corvettes, doesn't mean he has any interest in the electric Volt or the micro sized Aveo, any more than someone who buys Tide is likely to buy Pantene. Each micro-niche is there within social media and needs to be respected for what it is.

As solo business owners the big mistake is posting personal information about you and your life that isn't related to your business purpose and helping others. I use a Facebook profile for family to share those kinds of things with and a page for the rest of the world including my clients.

Through the use of a Facebook Page I can use Facebook messenger.

I would bet that Facebook messages have become the world's largest private email service. I say this because I have several friends who are executives and celebrities who only contact me by phone, text or Facebook. Like me they get so much spam that they have someone else filter all of their email first. Facebook is spam free by definition. If I don't want to hear any more about your new chocolate flavored pizza, I can just unlike you and never hear from you again.

Google+ doesn't quite offer that level of filtering yet on the message side. The follows do work the same way though.

This is the second main key to understanding Social Media right here. You only get to send your message to people who are interested, and only interested people listen to your message. If you lose their interest, you lose the listener. You can't (yet) force them to see your message like posting it on a billboard.

Traditional advertising on billboards, signs, vehicle wraps and even direct mail depend on an attention grabbing visual to start the connection. Social Media only does that with one little part of the channel, pay per click or pay per view ads. Everything else is based on a solid connection with an engaged and therefore interested person. This is the secret power of Facebook, Google+ and all social media if you learn to use it correctly.

There are probably a few people wondering why I haven't talked about the "reach" of Facebook due to the very large number of users. This is the single biggest mistake in all business is trying to "reach" everyone. With social media, no business or celebrity has a message so engaging as to keep everyone listening for any length of time.

Think of Facebook and Social Media like a free multi-level marketing program for your business that you don't manage and you don't pay[1] for. Your mission is to get a small group of fans that have a hundred or more friends each. When you engage them, they will forward your message, and that is how you achieve reach. *You cannot achieve reach in social media by trying to directly connect with everyone.*

Even the biggest celebs and most powerful executives have a few people they know are "in the know" that they watch for quick tips. Those "in the know" people are your ultimate connection.

Alert Service - Alert Services are one of the most cost effective tools out there for monitoring your status on the internet. Even if you hire out your SEO, Social Media or online advertising, I suggest an alert service. Every time your company is mentioned, you get an alert.

Google has a free alert service for members. It isn't as clean as the paid services, but it is free and every business should be using a service.

Facebook Profile - Every human on earth can have a Facebook profile. Until just recently you could have several. You could be your own Dr. Jekyll and Mr. Hyde. I could be an airline pilot on one profile, and be an author-business coach on another, and a Realtor© on yet another.

---

[1] Ethical Bribes and Rewards should never be overlooked, and are covered later.

Today the rules have changed and unless you cheat, just like there is only one you, there is only one profile that represents you. All of this is done in the name of transparency. Also you can only be you. No funny names like "Top Gun Scott" or "Speedway Champion" Only your name.

Your profile can be either personal or business. Facebook wants it to be personal. Mine is 90% business with 10% personal just so people know that I am a real human and I do have a little fun. I rarely check in anywhere until I leave because I enjoy some privacy.

Recently a guy asked me to send him a signed book for free because we checked into the same place on Foursquare. It was a little weird. Since I am in marketing I always check in at all of my clients and leave an online advice "tip" every time.

The good news is your profile is private only to people you are friends *with unless you make your posts public*. You choose who gets to see what you post. The reality is, if you post something that should not be seen by the world, someone will repost it publicly.

Because Facebook really is a pretty decent messaging tool instead of email, many people are starting to use their profiles more. After all, you can't get a message from someone who isn't your friend. Therefore you don't get spam.

Your Facebook profile is a way for you to share big events with lots of people quickly. Some famous people, like infomercial king Dean Graziosi, have (had?) two profiles, one for family, and one for customers. That isn't allowed any more. There is a new feature called subscribers instead.

There are still many businesses out there with a profile, and Facebook is cleaning them up slowly. If you have a profile for your business, get ahead of the game and change it to a *page* that connects to, and is managed by your personal profile.

So what does someone do who is a mild mannered reporter by day and super hero small business owner at night? They create Facebook *pages*.

Facebook Friend - A Friend on Facebook is someone who has requested to be able to see your Facebook Profile, and you have approved them. Friends can see just about everything you post on Facebook. Google+ created circles so you can restrict what others see based on the "circle" you put them in. Your mom never needs to see the photo of your new Tattoo is the theory. It doesn't work though.

Your friends always tell their friends who tell your family circle, so don't ever think anything on Facebook or any other Social Media site is private.

Facebook did just add a new feature called lists. You can sort your friends by lists like "Close Friends", "Family" or "Friends Except Acquaintances".

As part of lists, a brand new feature being launched now for public people – which you are if you own a business – is to allow *subscribers*. It is a limited friend, similar to "acquaintance" on Google Circles. I highly suggest using this feature so that anyone can follow you personally and you can more easily manage your friend list.

Every person's profile is limited to just 5000 friends. After all who really has that many people they know and want to talk too?

Facebook Subscriber – Subscribers are people you don't really know that want to keep up with what you post. Even though you might not have a goal of sharing updates with a broader audience, I suggest using both a page and subscribers to maximize your reach.

From the Facebook help file:

If your goal is to share updates **from your personal timeline** with a broader audience, allowing subscribers is a good option. When you allow subscribers, anyone can subscribe and get your public updates in their news feed, even if you're not friends on Facebook.

You can have an unlimited amount of subscribers, and subscribe to as many as 5000 people. (You can have 5000 friends on your personal account.)

Facebook Page - A Facebook page is a free (for now) public website created using a single Facebook template. *It is fully indexed by Google, and open for the world to see.* If that doesn't seem important, read it again. This is the best SEO work you can have done and it is FREE. Unlike your profile, your page can have unlimited followers or "likes".

www.facebook.com/bourquingroup
is my company's page

and

www.facebook.com/CakeTahoe
is a client page.

My business manages both pages and the owner of Cake Tahoe is also an administrator of the Cake Tahoe Facebook page just like I am an administrator of the Bourquin Group page. She and anyone in her shop she designates can post on the page as "Cake Tahoe" or as themselves.

With a page you can let anyone post, only let fans post or don't allow any posts except by administrators or managers. I encourage you to let anyone post. If you get spammed by another business or a competitor, it is pretty easy to remove, and the best part of the community aspect of Facebook and social media is spamming doesn't work, so it doesn't happen that often anyway.

If you have a business with several different products or services, you can create a page for each service. Again these are free, so I highly encourage you to look at your business carefully and see if more than one page isn't called for.

Although still a bit buggy, there are some new features so if someone else builds you a page because they couldn't find your page, you can claim it and combine it with your existing page. Sometimes the *likes* combine and sometimes you lose the *likes* from one page. Most of the time there are duplicates so you at least lose a few.

Facebook Place - Simply a page for a physical business where people can check in. When you create a page you will have options for what type of page you are creating. When you select a business place you are creating a Place page. For our purposes the only difference is Facebook users can "check in" with a smart phone when they are there.

Facebook Posts – Simply put this is something that you put on your timeline. It can be a picture, something you write, a link to a website, a place or an event.

Your friends can post on your timeline also. With a Facebook Page, you want your fans to post great stuff because it means you don't have too.

Facebook Likes - Generally just called a *"Like"* on Facebook.   Facebook Likes are simply a vote of confidence from a fan. They click the "like" button and you get a number.   You can't stop anyone from "liking" your page.   You may never meet these people and they don't have to be clients or even in your country.

Likes may or may not be a real customer or even a real fan.   I used to sell Porsche cars, I currently have a client that services out of warranty (ok used) Porsche Cars and I am a "fan" who has "liked" Porsche, but I don't currently, and in fact never owned a Porsche but I am counted as a "like" on the Porsche fan page.

If you buy *likes*, 80% of the people that "like" your Facebook page won't be real important to your actual business.   Most of your followers won't be engaged and you won't reach your target audience.

In the automotive segment my interests, people who sort of like cars watch what I say because they know I am a car nut.   I race LeMons[2] cars, have owned several muscle cars, classics and sports cars, and drive other peoples cars around race tracks when they are not comfortable going that fast on their own.

When my friends see that I "like" Porsche, they will ask me for my thoughts. I am a guy Porsche wants engaged

---

[2] I'l give Jay and Nick a plug here because it is so much fun www.24hoursofLeMons.com

even though I don't own one.   Again, social media marketing is different.

I also "like" Ford, and I have had lots of them, Mustangs, Pinto's (poor college days), Rangers and currently an F-150. I am quite engaged at Ford because I like the new CEO and the new cars.   The Focus electric looks like a great small electric.   The next Fusion, designed by the team that did the Aston Martin makeover before Ford sold Aston, is also a head turning car. I am considering a 2013 Fusion Plug in Hybrid, but I am not committed to it, and my 2003 F-150 is doing just fine 10 years later.

This may seem like I am the guy both Ford and Porsche should ignore. Instead the rules of Social Media Marketing dictate that I am the guy they want in the conversation. I talk about cars, talk to car people and look at cars every single day I am not on a cruise ship and even then I am thinking about cars.

Even writing a book on Social Media and Facebook I think about cars. Car companies need to engage car guys and car girls, not everyone.   The fans will influence their friends. _Reach_ is the brass ring here.

If you own a pizza place, engage foodies, if you are an actor who does drama, engage book and movie fans. The real secret here is to know what your friends and fans trust you for, that is what keeps them engaged.

If you are known as the best dresser among your friends, then you should *like* clothing related sites your friends might like. This builds your influence, and teaches you how to think like the people who might share your product or service.

Knowing the top of your social media multi-level pyramid and keeping them engaged is the real secret to success in social media. If your topic also happens to be something you are well known for all the better for you! Think of it as being rewarded for being you in your business.

We'll talk more about how to make those connections in Section III but don't skip Section II.

Many business owners mistakenly equate "likes" with social media success. Someone who *likes* you isn't necessarily engaged with you and they may not even care about you. They might just *like* you because their "friends" did and it was the cool thing to do in that social media community.

Just as there are millions of social media users, there are millions of social media communities. Most people are members of several "communities". The ties are very loose, and can be broken at any time for any number of reasons. This is why engagement is so critical to success and why buying *likes* isn't a long term option.

Facebook Like Button – That cute little thumbs up logo we all have seen somewhere. The funny part is how many small businesses use this wrong.

If you have a website, this should be how many people like your website, not your Facebook Page and vice versa. If you set it up wrong, every time someone likes your website, they might send a link that they just liked your Facebook Page.

This is a subtle and important thing to understand. In social media, nobody wants to look stupid to all of their friends. If you put the like button that links to your Facebook Page on your website, and the person has never seen your Facebook Page, they may be embarrassed, and you lost a Like, and possibly a customer or worse, an influencer.

Make sure the like buttons you use are attached to the correct website, page or profile before you leave them there.

Facebook Mention – In a post you can automatically link to other people, places and pages on Facebook with a mention. The way to do this is simply to use the @ sign before the person, place or page you want to mention like @Bourquin Group.

If Bourquin Group allows it (we normally do) then your post also shows up on our timeline. It is a great way to share credit for things you do with other businesses like sponsoring events.

If someone posts something you don't like you can have it removed.

UnLiked – When a person who is counted as a "*like*" on your Facebook page selects *unlike* and your count goes down.

Let's say the chef at your favorite restaurant left, you might *unlike* the restaurant and *like* the new place the chef is working.

Facebook Timeline - Timeline is the new format for Facebook profiles and pages. Personally I like the new format, but there are a few annoying things geared towards teenagers. For instance there is a great photo edit feature that lets you post a background picture and your photo floats on top. The background is called your "Cover Photo".

By itself this feature is great, but every time you change your profile picture or cover photo Facebook sends out a notice to all of your Facebook Friends. That might be cool for a tween, but 30-50 year old business owners I deal with call it SPAM. Don't change your picture daily unless there is a purpose to the new picture.

Google+® - Google+ is just another one of thousands of social media sites around the world. As Google+ adds features to try and hold off smaller sites like Yelp! and Angies List, and keep up with the social behemoth that is Facebook, Google+ gets more complicated and might alienate some users.

As a business owner this is a challenge because there is so much happening, you can get distracted by the noise and forget why you are spending any time with Google+ in the first place.

Google+ much like Facebook is a very underutilized tool in every businesses marketing arsenal.

After you have built your Facebook profile and page, do the same on Google+. Think of it like catering to PC users first , the bigger social market, and then adding the Mac Users, the smaller and more direct market.

All of the same rules of Facebook pages apply to Google+.

Google uses Gmail as a messaging platform and has some internal ways to "connect", it isn't as robust or trusted as Facebook Messages. Google + users can still bulk mail and spam when using Gmail accounts.   This feature means that Google won't get the depth of Facebook Messages any time soon.

This is the second main key to understanding Social Media right here. You only get to send your message to people who are interested, and only interested people listen to your message.   If you lose their interest, you lose the listener. You can't (yet) force them to see your message like posting it on a billboard.

Traditional advertising on billboards, signs, vehicle wraps and even direct mail depend on an attention grabbing visual to start the connection. Social Media only does that with one little part of the channel, pay per click or pay per view ads. Everything else is based on a solid connection with an engaged and therefore interested person. This is the secret power of Google+ and all social media if you learn to use it correctly.

There are probably a few people wondering why I haven't talked about the "reach" of Google+ due to the very large number of users.   This is the single biggest mistake in all business is trying to "reach" everyone. With social media, no business or celebrity has a message so engaging as to keep everyone listening for any length of time.

Think of Google+ and Social Media like a free multi-level marketing program for your business that you don't manage and you don't pay[3] for. Your mission is to get a small group of fans that have a hundred or more friends each.   When you engage them, they will forward your message, and that is how you achieve reach. *You cannot achieve reach in social media by trying to directly connect with everyone.*

Even the biggest celebs and most powerful executives have a few people they know are "in the know" that they watch for quick tips. Those "in the know" people are your ultimate connection.

Google+ Profile - Every human on earth can have a Google+ profile. Unlike Facebook, Google+ will still let you have several profiles. You could be your own Dr. Jekyll and

---

[3] Ethical Bribes and Rewards should never be overlooked, and are covered later.

Mr. Hyde. I could be an airline pilot on one profile, and be an author-business coach on another, and a Realtor© on yet another.

Your profile can be either personal or business. Google doesn't have the restrictions (yet) that Facebook does. My Google+ Profile is a mirror of my Facebook profile and I suggest that is how you approach it.

The good news is your profile is private only to people you are friends with, similar to Facebook *unless you make your posts public.* You choose who gets to see what you post. The reality is, if you post something that should not be seen by the world, someone will repost it publicly.

There are still many businesses out there with a profile instead of a page, and Google+ is likely to follow suit and limit that ability.   Even if they don't the markets are beginning to expect it.   If you have a profile for your business, get ahead of the game and change it to a *page* that connects to, and is managed by your personal profile.

So what does someone do who is a mild mannered reporter by day and super hero small business owner at night? They create Google+ pages. **The advantage to a page for business is the ability to claim the place and allow check in's. You can't "check in" at a profile with your smart phone.**

Google+ Friend - A Friend on Google+ is someone who has requested to be able to see your Google+ Profile, and you have approved them.   Friends can see just about everything you post on Google+.   Google created circles so you can restrict what others see based on the "circle" you put them in.   Your mom never needs to see the photo of your new Tattoo is the theory.   It doesn't work though.

Your friends always tell their friends who tell your family circle, so don't every think anything on Google+ is private.

Google+ Circles– Google has three default groups for you to put people in.   Friends, Acquaintances, and Public are the three default circles.   You are also allowed to define your own circles with Google+.   You could make one for Family and another for College Friends only.   It can get very complicated keeping track of all of these circles.

For business owners, we suggest that you keep it simple, friends only on your profile, and keep your "followers" on your pages.

Google+ Page - A Google+ page is a free (for now) public website created using a single Google+ template. *It is fully indexed by Google, and open for the world to see*.   If that doesn't seem important, read it again.   This is the best SEO work you can have done and it is FREE.   Unlike your profile, your page can have unlimited followers or "likes".   The difference is you can't (yet) get an easy to remember name for your Google + Page.

https://plus.google.com/113038827313228381201/posts
is my companies page

and

https://plus.google.com/105605036697614338309/posts
is the page for Cake Tahoe

My business manages both pages and the owner of Cake Tahoe is also an administrator of the Cake Tahoe Google+ page just like I am an administrator of the Bourquin Group page. She and anyone in her shop she designates can post on the page as "Cake Tahoe" or as themselves.

I used the same two examples in the book "How To Market On Facebook For Free" so you can easily compare the differences between a Facebook Page and Google+ Page.

With a page you can let anyone post, only let followers post or don't allow any posts except by administrators or managers. I encourage you to let anyone post. If you get spammed by another business or a competitor, it is pretty easy to remove, and the best part of the community aspect of Google+ and social media is spamming doesn't work, so it doesn't happen that often anyway.

If you have a business with several different products or services, you can create a page for each service. Again these are free, so I highly encourage you to look at your business carefully and see if more than one page isn't called for.

Google is better about letting you claim and own your page.

Google+ Place - Simply a page for a physical business where people can check in. When you create a page you will have options for what type of page you are creating. When you select a business place you are creating a Place page.   For our purposes the only difference is Google+ users can "check in".

Google+ Posts – Simply put this is something that you put on your timeline. It can be a picture, something you write, a link to a website, a place or an event.

Your friends can post on your timeline also. With a page you want your fans to post great stuff because it means you post less.

Google+ Follow - Generally just called a *"Follow"* on Google+, it is nearly identical to a Facebook "Like". Follows and Likes are simply a vote of confidence from a fan. They click the "follow" button and you get a number. You can't stop anyone from "following" your page.   You may never meet these people and they don't have to be clients or even in your country.

Follows may or may not be a real customer or even a real fan. I used to sell Porsche cars, I currently have a client that services out of warranty (ok used) Porsche Cars and I am a "fan" who has "followed" Porsche, but I don't currently, and in fact never owned a Porsche but I am counted as a "follow" on the Porsche fan page at Google+ and "Like" on the Facebook Fan Page.

Since Google+ isn't the mammoth that Facebook is, finding ways to "buy" follows aren't yet as easy as buying fake "likes" on Facebook. We experiment with "buying" likes on a regular basis, and so far all of the "likes" are fake profiles and we don't recommend the practice on Facebook nor will we when Google+ Follows hit eBay.

For more reasons why you want Follows from non-customer, read the section above on Facebook Likes.

Knowing the top of your social media multi-level pyramid and keeping them engaged is the real secret to success in social media. If your topic also happens to be something you are well known for, then all the better for you! Think of it as being rewarded for being you in your business.

We'll talk more about how to make those connections in Section III but don't skip Section II.

Many business owners mistakenly equate "likes" with social media success. Someone who *likes* you isn't necessarily engaged with you and they may not even care about you. They might just *like* you because their "friends" did and it was the cool thing to do in that social media community.

Just as there are millions of social media users, there are millions of social media communities. Most people are members of several "communities". The ties are very loose, and can be broken at any time for any number of reasons. This is why engagement is so critical to success and why buying *likes* isn't a long term option.

Google+ Follow Button – Again following the problems with the "like" button on Facebook, the "follow" on Google+ has a correct and incorrect usage.

If you have a website, this should be how many people like your website, not your Google+ Page and vice versa. If you set it up wrong, every time someone likes your website, they might send a link that they just liked your Google+ Page.

This is a subtle and important thing to understand. In social media, nobody wants to look stupid to all of their friends. If you put the Google+ button that links to your Google+ Page on your website, and the person has never seen your Google+ Page, they may be embarrassed, and you lost a Like, and possibly a customer or worse, and influencer.

Make sure the Google+ buttons you use are attached to the correct website, page or profile before you leave them there.

Google+ Mention – In a post you can automatically link to other people, places and pages on Google+ with a mention. The way to do this is simply to use the @ sign before the person, place or page you want to mention like @Bourquin Group. This is exactly the same on Facebook.

If Bourquin Group allows it (we normally do) then your post also shows up on our timeline. It is a great way to share credit for things you do with other businesses like sponsoring events.

If someone posts something you don't like you can have it removed.

UnLiked – When a person who is counted as a *"like"* on your Facebook page selects *unlike* and your count goes down.

Let's say the chef at your favorite restaurant left, you might *unlike* the restaurant and *like* the new place the chef is working.

UnFollow - If the "follower" clicks the Google+ Follow button again, they unfollow and your follow count goes down.

Influencer - These are the people who are most active and *trusted* in the social media world. Trusted is the keyword here, not active. There are paid fakers who make thousands of posts and claim thousands of friends yet can't lead starving children to McDonalds. A real influencer is the person who finds something they like and tell their friends. Those people come to your website or your Google+ page or better yet your business.

Keyword (Keyword Phrase)- Keyword and Keyword Phrase are interchangeable in today's online marketing world. A phrase just means more than one word. Instead of "coffee", the keyword phrase would be "organic fair trade coffee".

The **One Thing** that your business does is your primary keyword and the root word of your keyword phrase. Without it, you are just spending money.

Keywords are how people search for a business or information online. Keyword Phrases are a series of Keywords tied together to narrow the search.

"*Coffee*" can be a Keyword, and a very difficult one for any business to appear on page one of Google Search. "*Coffee Shop*" would be a short keyword phrase and only slightly easier to appear on page one of a search engine. "*Organic Coffee House in Huntington Beach*" could be a keyword phrase with only a dozen or so competitors.

The cost and effort required for becoming number one or even getting a spot on page one for a single keyword or a keyword phrase is basically based on three things:

First, is the market ratio. Basically you take the size of the market in monthly searches and actions and divide by how many competitors are in the same market space for those keywords. Google rates keyword competition as "low", "medium" or "high". Consider that your budget requirements.

Second, is finding out how much effort your competitors are putting into their SEO and SEM programs. This is a little bit like buying Yellow Pages ads. The business who spends the most money gets the biggest ad. The business that advertises with the best Yellow Pages book gets the best business. Spending the most with the best usually wins.

This leads to a question if you are going to hire someone else to do your SEO or Online Marketing work. Just as each Yellow pages only has one cover, one spine and one back, Google only has three spots on page one for Organic Search Results. Each SEO company can only get three businesses on page one.

Our policy is no more than two businesses per category in any geographic service area. Why?

As an example, let's say I focus on bakeries, and there are seven good ones in Huntington Beach. If all seven of them hire me to get them the best search results for the money, which three really get the best? There is only room for three.

Instead our business focuses on each region and seeks just one or two businesses per category to make sure they are getting the best service for the money.

The question to ask is, "How many of my competitors do you have as customers, and how many will you accept?"

Third is simply the quality of your website or landing page as it relates to that keyword. If you are trying to be number one for the keyword "Coffee" and you have a website about racing junk cars, your quality score will be very poor.

If you have a website or landing page dedicated to "Organic Coffee" and you are located in Huntington Beach, CA you have a better chance at earning a higher quality score.

MySpace - MySpace is the original social media site that really started to go for a mainstream appeal. in 2006 it was the most visited website in the world surpassing even Google. That was then, this is now. In 2012 it is still the 161st highest ranked website. Likely much higher than Google+ if you could separate Google+ from Google.

When MySpace was acquired by News Corp in 2008 for upwards of $500 Million it was big news that quickly fizzled. Today, MySpace has experienced a minor resurgence with the purchase by Specific Media LLC and Justin Timberlake.
Like all business that gains a direction and focus, MySpace has bounced off of its internet bottom.

Today MySpace is very focused on the music and pop culture and is a favorite area for stars and star gazers. If you are in an entertainment or fashion business MySpace may be a site you need to use. Because it serves such a niche market I won't cover it depth here. MySpace will require different handling given it's focus on the entertainment industry.

MySpace allows musicians to add fans as friends at any time. If you are a musician or are in the music business, you should start with MySpace and connect it to your Facebook account.

There aren't business pages on MySpace, mostly because the artist's profiles are the pages. Given the focus on the entertainment industry, it is a very smart move on the part of MySpace.

If you used MySpace in the past, take a look again. September and October 2012, MySpace did a complete rewrite, and the site can be quite entertaining.

Organic Ranking - Based on the quality of your website, your participation in the internet, the reach and influence your website has a score is compiled that creates the score that sets your position on search engines when someone types those keywords into the search box. The same thing happens with your Google+ Page when someone searches on Google+.

Paid Ranking - Your position as it relates to other advertisers. Largely based on the amount you will pay with a factor for quality included. When you set your PPC or CPM bid you decide where your ad will land. For enough money any ad can appear on Page One of just about every search engine for any keyword on any given day.

Many marketing companies who charge a fixed percentage of ad budgets will use this technique to run your ad rates up and make sure your budget is completely used. Make sure you get a keyword report and make sure they amount per click is a number that you can convert into a customer profitably.

Reach - Google+ Reach in basic Google+ terms refers to the number of people who see your posts on any given day. You might have 500 *likes* on your *page*, and 20 Influencers in that group. Your reach can hit several thousand or more if your posts are engaging and worth sharing. If your influencers *like* your Google+ Page Post, and they forward the post, it can go <u>viral.</u> I have had this happen twice. We hit several thousand views per hour with an article on <u>www.BeachStreetNews.com</u> and hit a *reach* of 100,000 with a *post* on the Bourquin Group *page* on Google+.

PPC or Pay Per Click - A method of paying for online ads. Each time someone clicks you pay a fee. Some clicks can be as little as two cents and others can be as high as $100. Truck Accident Attorney in California varies from $55-$100 a click on Google. Google+ and many social media sites have this as an option to pay for advertising. When testing new ads, I prefer this method because if I write a bad ad, and nobody clicks it, it doesn't cost me or my customer anything.

Landing Page - A landing page in Search Engine Optimization or Search Engine Marketing terms is a single web page that is dedicated to a very specific purpose. For instance TruSpeed Motorwerks might have a single web page just for Carbon Fiber Brake upgrades. PPC or CPM ads for brake upgrades would go directly to this "landing page". Think of it like looking for a Tiki Bar in the yellow pages and when you ask, you open right up to the best Tiki Bar Page.

The major search engines give you quality credit if your ad and your landing page are focused on the same topic or keyword phrase. In this case Carbon Fiber Brakes. If the ad went to a general service page that didn't mention Carbon Fiber Brakes until the bottom of the page after Oil Changes and Factory Service, a competitors ad might get placed first if he had a landing page just for Carbon Fiber Brakes because his quality score would be better.

There is a way to set a TAB page in Google+ to be a landing page for ads in Google+. This is a more advanced technique and will be covered in the full Social Media Book.

Search Engine Marketing – Commonly called SEM, this is simply the management of advertising on Search Engines and Directories. Like any advertising the quality of the ad will determine if you get the right customer. A good copywriter can say more in 70 characters than some people can say in a book.

Most search engines allow split testing. The means that you can run three ads for the exact same product, and they will tell you which one got the most clicks. Any decent ad program should include split testing with monthly removal of low performing ads.

Search Engine Optimization - More commonly called SEO; this refers to keeping a webpage focused on a specific keyword or phrase like "Oil Changes". A general page about Oil Changes, Brakes, Headlights and Tires isn't nearly as effective. The mindset is that if a customer searches for an Oil Change, they don't want to know about Tires, so the website that is most focused on Oil Change must be best.

Recent changes have altered this slightly because websites that don't offer oil changes, but offer advertising to places that do change oil were showing up first. Google considers those sites competition and is doing everything they can to prevent them from showing up first for free.

In the Appendix, there are a couple of examples of articles before and after applying traditional SEO methods. The main idea is your target keywords are clearly contained and used in a normal context within the article or copy.

CPM or Cost Per Mil - In finance a mil is a thousand so CPM is really CPT or Cost Per Thousand. This method of paying for ads charges for every 1000 times your ad appears on a user's screen. Rates appear much lower than PPC and can be as low as ten cents for 1000 views.

If you have a great attention grabbing ad that ends up in front of the right prospects this is a very cost effective method to market online.

Click Thru Rate or CTR – This is very simply the percentage of people who see your ad and click on it. Normal rates for a good ad are .01% to about 2.5%. The best ad I have seen written had a 3.5% rate. There are claims online of 5% and 10% CTR, and I haven't seen them. Given the size of Google+, 2% CTR can be a HUGE number of people. Many owners see .0275% and get discouraged. Don't. Think of it like a bus stop ad, how many people drive by and never even see it?

CTR is best used to compare two ads. If you write two ads, and one has a CTR of .1% and the other is .2%, scrub the ad performing at .1% and keep writing until you get one that does better than .2%. If you are paying for ads, you should be testing and tracking for improvement all the time.

Ethical Bribe - Not a Google+ staple yet, the Ethical Bribe is an offer of information, service or product in exchange for something from the person looking at your web site or Google+ Page. Normally you are asking them to join an email list and want their email address. Jeff Walker has built a small empire teaching people about the importance of lists.

The List - In the world of Internet Presence for conducting business, *the list* is your list of customers, and most of the time it is those customers whose email address you have on file and haven't asked to be removed from your list or unsubscribed from you mailings.

There are three parts to this list. The best is customers who recently bought, they are the hot prospects. Second is people who have been on the list a long time and maybe bought once before. Third are the new additions. They haven't bought anything yet, they liked your ethical bribe enough to stay on the list and haven't been asked to be removed yet.

Many business owners mishandle the list thinking the new customers are the important ones. The reality is it is the buyers that are the important ones. The more they buy the more they trust you and the more likely they are to buy again.

Building and maintaining your list is one of the most important tasks of Internet Marketing. For information and direct online marketing businesses list management is the make or break task. For a brick and mortar business, a great list can catapult you right over the top. Abusing the list can make your list disappear quickly.

Squeeze Page - Not traditionally associated with Social Marketing, a squeeze page is a place for you to post some information or a video and *squeeze* an email address or other information out of a customer in exchange for information they want. You offer an ethical bribe. You see these all the time and probably don't even realize what it is.

A Squeeze page is a very effective method of building a list of new potential customers via email and Social Marketing efforts and is best used before a new product or service is launched up to the actual product launch. Once the product is launched if it is a great product people won't need information, they'll buy.

The real reason to get out information early is to get feedback and find out what people want.

Viral - When talking about a video, picture or a post that goes way beyond your normal sphere of online influence, it is said to have gone viral. I am sure that someone has a specific number, but for my purposes, any time the Reach hits 100 times the number of Likes, it will fit our definition of Viral.

Internet Directories - Internet Directories are simply servers that list hundreds, thousands or even millions of websites. Some specialize in a niche giving them more weight in search results if your business is listed. There are a few key directories to get your site listed on in order to help your position in search engine results. If you want to get into as many directories as possible, hire an SEO or buy software or membership in a submission system.

DMOZ - DMOZ is the most widely regarded internet directory. It requires manual submission, and acceptance by a human so it could take months. You have to keep checking to see if you make it. Because of the human element, spam or domaineer sites aren't allowed.

Domaineering - The practice of speculating on domains. This practice has grown to attempting to control search results and funnel them to a specific domain. Some call these "spam" domains because they don't have any useful information. Just paid links to other domains. Google is actively seeking to limit this practice mastered and once nearly totally controlled by Kevin Ham M.D. in 2007[4].

Aggregator - A company that is a single point of reference for hundreds of websites. They attempt to dominate a keyword in search results. The idea being two fold. People searching only find the aggregator site, and people who want to be found must pay to be on the site. Some are attempting to work and act like paid local directories.

Local Directories - A local directory is a smaller search engine within a niche. Some have a social aspect to them like Foursquare and others are very business oriented like DMOZ. Think of the local directories like a custom yellow pages based on where you are. Normally they will use the location of a smart phone to guide you to what you are looking for nearby. Google created Google Local to do the same thing, scrubbed it and now has Google Places.

Yelp! - Yelp! is a local directory best known as a quick research tool for restaurants. Don't overlook Yelp! just because you aren't in the restaurant business. If your customers are checking Yelp!, you need to pay attention to Yelp!. The best advertising on Yelp! is check in deals on

---

[4]link http://money.cnn.com/magazines/business2/business2_archive/2007/06/01/100050989/

Mobile. If you are running a restaurant, buying a premiums listing might be a good idea. Again test everything.

Foursquare - Foursquare is a more social media focused local directory. It lists just about any brick and mortar business, and lets people share with their friends what is going on. I am sure the people at Yelp! and Foursquare would disagree, but they really do the same thing for non-restaurant businesses. Ideally you should engage on both Yelp! and Foursquare and test which brings in better results.

Manta - Manta is a business to business local directory. On occasion though, you might get some consumer business as someone is looking around. The basic premium listing is something worth testing for three or four months if your business serves business. The premium listing gets your competitors ads off of the page that displays your information.

SPAM - Saved for last, SPAM in the internet world is a very important topic. The short course is "don't do it". Companies that use the technique swear it works. The clients we work with who have tried it agree it doesn't.

Spam comes in many forms, but basically any bulk message system like email, social websites or texting can be used to send spam. The simple rule is "If it is only a sales pitch, then it is SPAM."

Don't get labeled a spammer, and don't let your company get labeled a spammer either It is NEVER good for business.

Mobile Friendly - The growth of mobile internet has made the biggest change in ten years at Google is the mobile rating.   If your website isn't mobile friendly, it doesn't matter how good your SEO is you go to the bottom of the list.

Mobile is a big reason why we use and recommend Wordpress for all of our clients.   Most of the templates automatically adjust to work correctly on mobile screens.

Podcasting - simply put podcasting is creating your own radio station online. It's very easy to do but beyond the scope of this book. If you visit easyguidebooks.com you will find The *Easy Guide to Podcasting*.

In the *Easy Guide to Podcasting* I cover very easy home setups including the exact model numbers of microphones, software and equipment that we use here and and our office and that I using use in my home.

Also in the *Easy Guide to Podcasting* is a step-by-step guide so that you can be online with your own program within just a few days.

IV. Social Media and Business

Social Media can be one of the most overlooked tools in a business's marketing **and** customer service tool box.   For years, businesses have been trying to teach professional sales people how to ask for the referral.   Social media when properly used can do it for you.

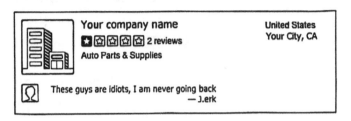

The two way channel of information from the customers is a huge bonus.   When a sales person calls for a referral and gets a cold response, they likely will never know why. With social media, all you have to do is read the comments, both good and bad.   A really good alert service will tell you anytime something is said.

As a consultant, it is amazing how many business owners and managers have never read the comments posted about their business anywhere online.   The reactions can be quite humorous.   Just about every business has one bad post, and those reactions of the owner when I present the complaint to them are the most interesting and telling about a business and it's owners or managers.

When the owner of a business reads a one star rating on a website and it says something like "This should have been a half star, but I can't go that low and I want people to know how bad this is.", the reaction of the owner tells me all I need to know to get started.

If the owner says "Wow, I never knew we were doing that, I need to fix it right now." The owner is on the right path when it comes to delivering value to the customer and will be on the right track with social media.

If the owner takes the other track and says something like "Some people are so difficult." and ignores the comments, you then have a challenge as a business consultant. Here is free feedback, the best kind of open, angry and honest feedback you can ask for and the owner is ignoring it. This is where a good consultant can be worth his weight in gold.

There are an entire list of businesses that can and do survive for many years with poor customer service, bad pricing strategies and poor product selections. They can also survive without listening to any customer at all other than to make change. Have you ever been to a convenience store with no other stores in the area. You and the clerk didn't share the same language, the place was a mess and yet you still bought something? We've all been there.

If survival is all you wanted out of your business, you wouldn't be reading this book.

Why is Social Media Important?

Social media connects many facets of life and business all in one nice neat box, or creates one big mess to fix. The business is 98% in control of which one happens if and only if they participate in social media.

If you don't participate, you are waiving your rights to control of the information about your company, and therefore allowing anyone else to take it from you. Ethics are not enforced on the internet so an angry customer, competitor or menacing teenager might be taking charge of your online presence. Fortunately many of the social sites are getting verification of the person's authority to build, post and control information about a business. Sometimes though those controls aren't much.

More importantly, 80% of the time when someone does online research, they will change their buying decision if there is an overall negative sentiment about a business or a product. Keeping those four star and five star ratings on yelp can help make a business.

Why is Social Media Exploding and Not a Fad?

Humans have a list of needs. Over the years these needs have been studied, documented and tested. One need that shows up time and time again is the need to belong. One of the four connecting triggers in sales is the need to belong. After all you don't want to be the only person on your block that doesn't have HDTV do you? How many times has that sales pitch worked.

The entire "Keeping up with the Joneses" consumerism depends on the social need to belong we share as humans.   There is a first group of consumers who are often called early adopters.   In "Crossing the Chasm", the early adopters are critical to getting a new service or product off the ground.   The early adopters are the consumer leaders and they are the white elephants[5] of Social Marketing.   When you reach this group, you reach thousands of others indirectly.

When one of these early adopters tries the new cupcake shop in town, they tell their friends.   If they like it, their friends go.   If they don't, business is lost.   They are the "Jones" everyone else wants to keep up with.

When he finds a new better place to get his car fixed, he tells his friends and they go.   When Mrs. Jones finds a new salon, she tells her friends and they go.

Before the social websites joined the internet, it might have taken months for a person to walk into a shop, buy a product, and then let a dozen or so people know about it.   Today, they can tweet it out to 3000 people in 10 seconds.

This is the awesome power of reach in Social Marketing.   Just like life, there are leaders and followers.   One of the great tricks of Social Marketing is to target and reach out to the leaders.   The followers come for free because they

---

[5] a "White Elephant" refers to a rare prize.   In financial sales it means a very wealthy client.   In marketing it is the lead buyer that you can't survive without.

want to *belong* to the leaders group, even if they never met the leader. This is why celebrity endorsements work.

Many of us are leaders in some areas and followers in others. In the world of technology, I tend to work from the position of a leader, having founded two different tech companies. Like most tech people, in the world of clothing and fashion I am clearly a follower. I get other people to put together my wardrobe.

For a company to market to me, and try and get me to buy clothes is a total waste of time and money. I tell them every time I go shopping, and yet I recall tossing several expensive glossy pictures from clothing stores into the recycle bin this week. If you want to sell me clothes, market to my wife. If you want to sell her a 80" LED Energy saving TV or a NEST smart thermostat, you better get to me. Know your customer.

With social media, you can market directly to influencers and for all practical purposes ignore the followers. They come with the territory if you reach and engage the influencers.

Social Marketing is about Engagement.

V. The Social Internet

Facebook didn't invent Social Marketing or social media. There were several key players that came first such as MySpace. Even email can be considered a form of social media because people can forward email rather quickly and easily to a large number of people who trust them.

What Facebook did for social media is twofold. First, Facebook took social media mainstream and outflanked MySpace by keeping to the basics that customers were really looking for. Musicians and kids like the features of MySpace, but the clear winner for users is Facebook.

Second, Facebook found a way to build a separate and totally controlled internet. Instead of email you send "messages". Since you can't send bulk messages, there is no spam (yet) and you can block just about anyone from sending you a message. I communicate with several high level players through Facebook exclusively. If I email them, I'll get no response. Facebook message them and I have an answer in minutes.

Facebook also built a mini-internet hosting system for businesses with *Facebook Pages*. Each page is really a website within Facebook that is visible to the outside world. Unlike your profile, a Facebook Page is open and indexed by the search engines. For a startup business that can't afford a website, Facebook gives them space to build a website and have a shot at being found on Google, Bing and Yahoo.

When people feel like their groups are safe, they are more willing to share and listen to ideas. When there isn't any spam or unsolicited email, the assumption is that everything in the inbox is worth reading. I don't know about you, but I get 6000 emails every day. I read less than 20 of them. I only get about a dozen Facebook Messages each day and read them all.

Apple has just added a cool e-mail filter with iOs 6 on the iPhone and iPad to try and catch up. You can now designate people as "VIP" so you can quickly check to see if you have received an important email. All of my family, close friends and clients are on the VIP list. In one glance I can look at my phone and know if there is anything I should pay attention too. It isn't as clean as messages but it is a good start. If I could just get graphics in my Apple Mail signature line....

Facebook messages created a "VIP" type list a long time ago. If I approve you as a friend, you can send me a message. If you are a "subscriber", you can't interrupt my day or send me spam.

Most business owners don't think of themselves as public figures when they start out so this doesn't seem that important to them. As their business grows they realize they are public people and appreciate the ability to filter out the noise.

Filtering out the noise is what makes Social Marketing different from traditional marketing. Your targets have the choice to tune you out in a way that TiVO can only dream of. They don't just skip your commercial; they never have the chance to see it in the first place if they don't want to.

This filtering is also the magic of Social Marketing. If you engage the influencers, you are no longer spammy or tuned out. Instead because your influencer targets are engaged, they forward your message as if it was their own. If the recipient doesn't approve, you aren't the one they block. The influencer is. Since influencers don't like to get blocked they are very careful about what they forward.

Social Marketing is about reaching out to the right people and engaging them in a way that convinces them to reach out to their followers. This is why asking for the sale directly is difficult and less beneficial. When you ask for the sale, you are only asking your fans. When you ask for the referral, you could get a hundred fold more potential customers. Those are the home runs you read about that companies like Stamped (recently purchased by Yahoo) tout so loudly.

If you still aren't sure about using Social Media as a marketing tool for your business, all I can say is keep reading, invest a couple of hours and see for yourself. You might get more business, and you might not. My bet is you will (over time) gain loyal customers and fans. The more you give them, the more you will get back.

VI. Build Your Foundation

This book won't cover every social website out there, simply because the landscape changes way to quickly. Instead, what you get here is a step by step guide for the major players, and a simple to follow checklist that you can use with any website other than Facebook, Google+ and MySpace. Those three are different because you have some creative ability to control your page. Other sites might let you soon, but for now they are pretty easy form submissions.

Before you get started, you really should have some things ready to go. It will make the entire process go faster. In order to help you build your Social Media "package" and get you ready to launch your online presence there is a little business coaching that needs to happen. If you get stuck here, it is ok to get started and come back to the big items later. Look for another book in this series that will be dedicated to helping you really fine tune these big areas.

Building Your Social Media Package

To begin with, I suggest a note pad or a three ring binder to keep this all organized. When you are done you will have a pretty solid little book that other people can use to maintain your Social Media Presence and Marketing.

As with all things business, we will start with your customer. After all without them you don't have a business in the first place. Don't skim this section, it is the most important. If you write all of the answers out and put them in your Social Media binder, it will be much easer to succeed with Social Marketing.

Define your customer.

This step can be very challenging to many business owners, and the most common answer I get is "everyone". What you want to do is define your customer down to a single person. You want to know everything about them. This definition is your target influencer.

As an example, one client owned a small pizza restaurant, and he gave me the stock answer "everyone". So the conversation went like this:

Scott: Do you sell a Gluten Free Pizza?
Owner: No.

Scott: Do you sell anything Gluten Free?
Owner: No.

Scott: Is there anything a person on a Gluten Free Diet can eat here?
Owner: Not really, we sell pizza and pizza is bread.

Scott: So Gluten Free dieters are part of "everyone" and you just told me they aren't a potential customer?
Owner: Yea, I guess so.

The conversation went on for an hour, until we defined the single most profitable customer as: Male, with a car, who likes pizza, beer and live music, 24-34 years old, that works within a 10 mile radius, and is single.

Now we have a picture of a person to market too. This is important for the next step.   As you think about how to answer the question, sometimes it is easier to start by asking "who isn't your customer?" and then use that list to define your customer.

We aren't trying to define all of your customers, just those who are the best and most profitable to your business. In Social Media, they are the influencers that bring the other customers with them. Engage one, you sell hundreds, and that is what makes measuring social media so difficult.

Who is your customer?
Describe your one best customer here in as much detail as you can stand.

Identify Your Customers Problem.

Every business exists because it solves a real or perceived problem for its customers. When you can define your customer, you can get to know them, put on their shoes and learn their problems. When you do that, you can charge for the solution and that is how a business makes money. The better you know your customer, and the more closely aligned your solution is to the problem the more you can charge.

For the pizza place, the customer's problems are "single", "need to eat", "need to relax", "don't want to cook". The pizza place solves all but the "single" problem directly. Indirectly it can make the person feel less lonely by bringing in more people like him.

**What is the problem your customers have?
Write down "why" they need your business.**

Identify Your Solution

Now that you know your customer, and you know their problem:

What is your solution? (i.e. Pizza, Beer and Music)

How does your solution solve the customer's problem(s)?

i.e.   "Single" - lots of people, feeling of belonging

"Need to eat", "don't wan't to cook" - Affordable pizza Specials

"Need to relax" - Live Music and Happy Hour

About Your Business

This section seems obvious, but you would be amazed how many people enter different information on different websites, and pay us good money to go fix it because they are getting bad reviews for posting the wrong hours, or forgetting to update the new phone number. One business even moved just three blocks and thought a sign in the old window would be enough.

Every time any of this information changes, fix it in your Social Media binder and on all of the websites you participate on.

Business Legal Name:

Business Trade Name or DBA:

Business Address:

Hours: Mon
            Tues
            Wed
            Thurs
            Fri
            Sat
            Sun
After hours appointments?

Do all customers come to you, do you go to them or both?

200 word basic description of your business - This should be in the form of Problem - Solution - Call to Action

400 word full description - This can be either a four part sales letter where you state the problem the customer has - describe how you or your other customers have felt the same way - describe the solution you found or offer - Call to Action, i.e. enter email address, call, stop by, print coupon etc.

Put together a collection of 10-15 really good photos, your company logo and if appropriate a head shot of the owner or general manager. You don't want the first photo online of your business to be a drive-by picture from an old blurry cell phone that someone took when they showed up after hours and were angry that you were closed. That photo won't sell your business for you.

Put these photos on a CD or a thumb drive and keep them right in the binder. This way if your computer crashes, you get a new one or decide to work from a hotel, you can.

Gather Testimonials

If you have testimonials, that is great and you need to use them to kick start your Social Marketing campaign. If you don't have them, don't wait for them, get started and ask for testimonials as you go. Always ask when a customer leaves smiling. Never let them go without asking.

Put together a budget.

Believe it or not, if you only have time, you can do well in Social Marketing with a budget of zero. If you have some advertising money, buying some upgrades to your accounts and testing advertising is worth doing. Each site covered will have some notes about how our testing has gone with each of the sites as we have used them for clients in business.

Build Your Businesses Social Media Persona

Start by defining no more than three customer problems that you solve. The Bourquin Group has one real product. We help people and businesses find their one thing. We also help them market the one thing by offering SEO, Mobile &Local Marketing and Social Media Marketing. It all really starts with the consulting and coaching that are needed to define the one thing.

Without defining **the one thing**, we don't know who the customers is, where the company is going or why the two should ever meet., In order to define the flight path from customer to destination and make it profitable, we always start here.

Once you can identify your one thing then you can define no more than three problems you solve for your customers. Now you can give your business an online persona. What makes your business better or different? Why would a customer pick you over anyone else?

Use this information to write your story. Write it as if you are talking to your perfect customer. If you don't want to write it, you can hire it out, but make sure your writer knows your customer cold.

Now you can get to work.

VII. Step By Step Guide

The next step is to identify the sites you want to participate in and the sites that you will use for alert. Google alerts should be fine to get started.

Some sites like Facebook will require that you as a human have a profile before you can build the Businesses existence. Ideally you should treat every site as two entities, you and your business. Yelp! for example lets you build a business profile, but doesn't let you add multiple admins (yet).

Even for those sites, you should have a separate email address so you only need to memorize one username and password for all of the sites. We set up a Gmail account for every business client. They own the account, not us.

Since the password requirements are all different as well, I suggest using a spreadsheet and keeping it in the binder. Some sites require passwords with special characters, others don't even allow special characters.

As simple table like this will do just fine, it is what we use for our clients.

As you claim your business on different sites, you will find that they all verify businesses differently. Some will give you a code and you call them, others will give you a code and call you at the listed number. Finally you might get a post card or have to fax in a copy of business paperwork like a business license.

We don't keep any of the information about how we claim a business, but you might want to add it to your password table.

If you want to get super organized, then build a three ring binder with all of your information in it, your story, customer definitions and your site information. You will end up with an informal business plan, and most importantly, a plan that works.

Website	User name	email used	password
Facebook	scottb	social@email.com	pass123$
Google +	scottb	social@email.com	pass123$
Yelp!	scottb	social@email.com	pass123
foursquare	scottjb	social@email.com	Pass123$

If you noticed the username for foursquare being different, you are right. That happens because someone else might beat you to the username no matter how crazy you make it. That is why a simple table like this in your social media binder will make your life much easier.

Getting Online

With Google's latest changes, there are two ways for you to be found online. Well at least that is as far as search engine's go.

Choice number one just get all of your local listings correct and up-to-date. There are over 400 local directories that you will need to keep up with if you want to do this correctly. Heading minimum you should do the top 30 or 50. Most website hosting companies like ours offer a local listing management service at a very reasonable price.

Choice number two it Is to buy your way in either with paper click ads or buying a spot on the directory for your Business category.

Facebook

Facebook is a site that should be used by all businesses. Since it is clearly the big stick when it comes to social reach, no business can afford to ignore Facebook.

Facebook today is much bigger than it was a year ago, and several times bigger than it was when I built my first account. This is NOT going to be the answer everything guide to Facebook. What this is intended to be is a focused guidebook for business owners or managers who want to get better results from their Facebook usage as it relates to business. There are going to be a few "don'ts" and a few "do's". Only the key areas that you need to work in for business are going to be covered.

> **2015 Update Note -** *Facebook has become the biggest referral generator for digital publishers and is fast approaching that mark for many other businesses as well.*

You have a business to run and a life to lead. The idea here is that Facebook is a time killer if you don't use it right and at the same time you have to be the real you or your friends will abandon you. Starting with friends is the crux of any Facebook presence.

When I work with small business owners or teach my seminars I refer to Internet Presence often. Internet Presence for a small business like the girl who bathes my two Australian Shepherd dogs might only be a Facebook Presence. She just recently got an official listing on Yelp!. She is so busy even her Facebook Page is out of date.

We are going to start and focus on your Facebook Presence initially. If you don't have one, this will help you get started, if you do have one, I hope you will find some nuggets that you can use to make some significant improvements in the results you are getting for the time and effort you put in.

Your Facebook Profile

For a business owner who is working a small business on the side, this is the scariest place to be. Your boss and your job will eventually find out that you are moonlighting and advertising it on Facebook. Now that Facebook no longer allows dual profiles, you have a decision to make.

For established business owners, or people starting a new venture who are focused on that venture, this is an easy section to cover.

The first steps of this section are the basis of your Facebook marketing program.

Step One: Get a Facebook Profile - If you don't have one, you need one. You can't own the Facebook Page for your business if you don't. If you don't claim your Facebook Page and prove you own it, someone else can post incorrect information. Someone once saw my client walk into her bakery at 6 am, so until we claimed the Facebook Page for her, the hours said open at 6 am. Several customers weren't happy.

Getting a Facebook Profile is easy, just go to www.facebook.com right on the first page is the basic sign up form and a green button that says sign up. If you do it from a computer with a couple of good pictures you can upload, that is even better.

Step Two: Build Your Profile - Your Facebook profile needs to be the real you. A little personal history is fine but not too much. I have my college, high school, and military units posted to make it easier for any of those guys to find me and get in contact with me. Again, I don't waste time on Facebook reading peoples life stories every day. I just try to build a picture of who I am as a business owner and consultant and how I can help people and businesses.

Recently Facebook changed how its profiles and pages are viewed. The new format is called a Timeline. You get to have a background header photo and your photo on top. This is a great way to set up a visual image for people when they connect with you. If you are a baker, have your photo in your best chef's whites. If you own a music store, have a photo of the store.

My personal profile timeline shows me at different marketing events. My photo rarely changes and shows me outside doing something. The intent is to create a mental picture that I am outside and marketing for my clients all the time. Spend a little time thinking about your profile picture and cover photo and how they can help visually support your brand both personally and professionally.

As you build your profile always keep in mind three things, your brand, your business and your customer. If you aren't in the outdoor recreation business, don't post a hundred pictures of you and your family camping. Maybe just one to let people know you are real.

Customers are ruthless, they don't want to visit your office to find you out goofing off, they want to know you are always working to make their life better. Don't brag about how much time you don't work on Facebook. Even though the profile is private to the people you approve as friends, they can share it with their friends and it will come back to you like bad online karma.

Never Consider Anything On Facebook As "Private".

Now that you have built your Facebook profile, here are some tips on how to use it.

1. Check in at every business that you can where you know the owner and are friendly with them. Ask them to do the same.

2. "Like" all of those same businesses and ask them to do the same.

Facebook has some good apps for doing this right from your smart phone.

Step Three: Build a Page - This one is a little tougher. Your page is your website on Facebook and it might be the first and last impression of your business that people see so make it count. The worst part is that you might already have a Facebook page and not know it.

I have seen as many as four pages for the same business on Facebook and none of them were built by the owner or his employees. The task here is now to "claim" the pages as yours.   Once "claimed" you can hopefully combine them.

This is where you have to remember you aren't paying Facebook $19.95 a month for web hosting. So far all of this is free so it might take time. Recently while trying to combine three Facebook Pages into one for a client, Facebook let me claim all three, and then combine two. When I tried to add the third it took several weeks and emails with photos of the location and her business license and a phone call to the store to verify that I was in fact an "authorized party".

The funny thing is I showed up as the owner the next day on Facebook and it added it to my Facebook Profile Timeline. Those calls were interesting.

The way to get to Facebook support to combine pages if you don't have the menu option under your profile isn't easy. You will need to start with the help menu pull down. This is under the arrow to the right of your name at the very top of the screen. You will need to read all of the help file before being allowed to email the support desk. It isn't easy but remember, Facebook is still free.

If you type in "combine pages" it will get you to the right area.

My staff is all around the world so when we build Facebook pages and need to verify information it is a little more work than if you do it yourself I am sure.

If your business has five locations, build a separate page for each location.

The first step to building a page is to search for your business and see if anyone else has built one. Just type the name of your business in the search box while you are logged in. If there is already a page or a place that is your business, click on it. While on that page there should be a "claim this page" link. If not, you will need to copy the entire url from your browser window and send it to support to claim the page. Sometimes they just call, other times it has taken a week and they ask for copies of business licenses or other documents.

If there isn't a page already for your business or a place for your business, simply scroll to the bottom of your browser page and click on "create a page". Follow the step by step process to build your page. If you have any photos you can use, have them available to upload.

Fill out as much information in the Basic Information Section as possible. While you are in that section click each of the menu options on the left panel to get as much information online as possible.

The "cover photo" is the big wide picture. Take a look at: www.facebook.com/caketahoe to see how we used a cover photo of the shop and used the logo as the "profile" picture.

The more of this you get up now, the more likely you are to get Likes that stick.

Double check all of the simple things, like your address, phone number and hours. You would be amazed at how many people overlook that stuff.

Step Five: Get Liked - This is where you spend a little money for the first time. It is a dirty secret that you can buy likes. Your need likes to claim your own name on Facebook, and as of this writing there are thresholds of 30,50 and 100 that we have seen. You can buy ads on Facebook to get likes, or buy them on Ebay.

There is a huge first mover advantage here and it isn't just about customers. It is about clarity and confusion as well. If you own Joes Garage, and Joe owns a restaurant called Joe's Garage and he is first, you are going to start getting calls from confused restaurant suppliers.

You can get to 30 likes in about a day by either buying Pay Per Click or PPC ads on Facebook and selecting the button that says "Advertise where I am likely to receive Likes". and budget about $40. If you do this watch it closely, because you might get 30 likes in an hour for $10.

Another method of getting likes is the ethical bribe. Give a discount or deal to the first 100 people who like you and come in the shop. If you have a busy store, 30 likes won't take long at all. If you are an Internet Marketing Company where clients never visit your office, this method may not work.

Finally you can "buy" likes. go to eBay and search "Facebook likes" or "twitter fans". I don't personally ascribe to this method for small businesses, but we have seen it work and can give you the ability to grab your name quicker. Facebook seems to look the other way when it comes to faceless people who have dozens of accounts. You may as well use it to your advantage and get your name before someone else does.

For very small or very targeted niche, I don't like the idea of buying big numbers of fans because your real fans might take a look and see that your little shop of magic in Tempe Arizona has 800 fans in the Philippines and you don't sell online. Being fake won't fly for long on Facebook.

Step Six: Claim Your Page UserName – If you have a brick and mortar business that is verified, or after you have enough fans listed as *likes*, you can claim a "username" for the page.

The steps as of this writing are:
1. Log Into Facebook
2. On the Top Right, click on the down arrow to access the drop down menu.
3. Click on your Facebook Page.

4. When You page comes up select the "Edit Page" drop down near the top right.
5. On The Edit Page drop down select "Update Info"
6. The Fourth Item on that page should be Username: Select this area.
7. You will see a place to fill in your name. For Cake Tahoe, we chose CakeTahoe.

Like Google, Facebook is smart enough to parse out the words. Now you have a domain at Facebook you can advertise like facebook.com/CakeTahoe, ours is facebook.com/BourquinGroup.

Think carefully though, you are only allowed to change your username for your page one time.

The big advantage here is that these free pages on Facebook are fully indexed by Google. So you might think about using keywords for your page name instead of your business name. If you are Rudy's Garage and specialize in Custom Hot Rods, you might use a more complete name on Facebook like Rudy's Hot Rod Garage. Your Facebook domain would be facebook.com/RudysHotRodGarage.

Adding the keyword Hot Rod to your domain would help Hot Rodders find you and also help people know right away that you are not the same as Rudy's Garage that is foreign car specialist two towns over.

Once you claim your place double check the accuracy of everything and then use your smart phone to check in and establish your actual location.

Step Seven: Post - This is the step that causes the most confusion and frustration across the board with business owners, consultants and celebrities. If they turn over the responsibility too early, or without enough direction, the posts get out of hand and occasionally can offend people.

The photos and information on your Facebook Page should be geared around two areas. Photos and information about your staff will help your influencers feel "connected" to them. If someone has a baby and they are ok sharing it, share it.

The other area is about solving problems for your customers. Every business solves problems for customers and nothing else. Even the Chef at Cake Tahoe is solving the problem of the perfect cake for the perfect wedding, or the problem of what treat to give a child after an accomplishment or even a different kind of birthday party with cupcakes so some can have chocolate and others get vanilla.

Every time you post, are you connecting or problem solving? You should be, so if you aren't doing either, don't post. If you can't come up with at least one connection or problem solution each week, you need to slow down and listen to your customers. They have problems that will build your business. Your one thing is their solution. Trust me when I say, *your business problems won't build your business.*

If you delegate your social media posting and therefore your Social Marketing, make sure that the person or service you delegate to understands you, your purpose and direction, your business and your customer. Facebook is a tool for you to connect to your customer via your business. Never violate that trust and be very careful not to sever that connection unintentionally.

Posting is the place where each business gets a little different in how I advise people to post or to create TABS. So for this step and the next step, I will include some examples based on the size of the business. These are the last steps on your roadmap to success in Social Media as long as you stay honest with your fans and give them something worth sharing, you will see a difference in your business and you won't need to live online.

Creating Your Roadmap For Social Marketing Success:

Start by defining the one problem you solve better for people than anyone else.

Write it down so you look at it every time you post or add information to your page.

Think of a story that relates your solution to your customer's problem as they see it.

Put together the proof that you can solve it for them.

If you have a website, get the Facebook Like Button and the Google+ recommend button on there as quickly as possible. Ideally you would also link it to your Facebook page and Google Places Page.

If you want to get really advanced, you can have a feed from your Facebook Page or Google Page appear on your website. It just depends on your business and how much time you have to spend online.

The benefit of building it this way up front, is you only need to post a super deal once, and it appears on both or all three. The downside of course is over use and the potential of being labeled a spammer, and losing the engagement of your influencers.

Once every two or three months or anytime you make a major website change, make sure to update it on your Facebook Page via a link.

Once you have these items outlined, then you go to work on your page. Below are some guidelines to keep you on track with your business.

Solo Internet Marketer - If you are selling information online, you probably already have a a Facebook Page and have connected with other marketers. Buying and reviewing each other's information products online is a great way to build your testimonials and get customers buying. A great use of the TAB feature for this level is to create a Landing Page or a Squeeze Page here. Everyone really should look for a few of these sites to see how a Squeeze Page is done. If you ever want a successful e-mail campaign, a Squeeze Page is a great way to grow your list.

Actor/Celebrity/Author - The outline discussed in the previous section pretty well covers how to post on Facebook. The key is to remember who your fans are and what they get from following you. Normally cool points with their friends, a little influence and a feeling of being connected to someone bigger than themselves.

I think Actors and Celebrities can have the most fun on Facebook because they can go out and discover cool things to share.

Your goal as a celebrity is simply to build influence by doing or finding cool things to share with other people. Things that they want to share. It could be a charitable cause, or it could be a new earth saving solar technology. It doesn't matter as long as it is a subject that brings your fans together as a unified community. When you do that your influence grows and as they say "Your stock goes up, way up."

Some people in this category have figured out how to create a brand at the same time by leveraging their cool status and connecting it to their community.

Brett Michaels created a line of T-shirts he markets online including on his Facebook Page. Others endorse products or put their names on other peoples stuff and then pump up the product on their page.   The idea is that their followers want to be connected and also be more like them.

The potential here to build a name, a brand or a character while using Facebook as the conduit is quite extraordinary and limited only by your imagination.   The key here is to focus on a purpose or a connection and use that to the maximum without losing fans along the way.

Social Marketing by the Celebrity crowd can be forgiving to some extent. Where other markets, that isn't true.

Authors may have the toughest time because it is really about building a community for your fans.   The problem you solve is their common bond. On the other side of the coin, once the community is built it may give you the problems or stories for the next book. All you have to do is check in and listen to the fans.

Politician - President Obama and his team easily out flanked the GOP party and used Social Marketing as a key method of reaching influencers and creating a successful path to the White House. Anytime there is a hot topic, the President (then Senator) blasted out a quick message letting supporters know "I got this one". Instead of fanning the flames and creating mountains out of mole hill sized problems, the mole hill would just cave in.

Elections and the entire political process have been changed forever by Social Media, and more correctly by Social Marketing.

Unlike celebrities, Social Media can be very unforgiving of gaffes by politicians. Again direction, focus and vision need to be maintained. What problems are you going to solve for your voters and how. Getting elected and staying in office are just another form of salesmanship and Social Marketing is a tool no politician can survive without.

Using the tools incorrectly is equally dangerous. Sexting has killed as many political careers as Social Media has made.

Politicians can very effectively use the elements of celebrity and community to bring people together and create a cause they will want to share and influence.

The important thing is to have a clear vision of the cause or direction they can share.

Single Location Business - One Owner. One of the big problems facing the solo entrepreneur and business owner is the problem of running the business. Facebook isn't like the Yellow Pages where you have to meet with your rep once a year to make sure your ad is still ok.

Since small business is the core of the business world in the US, it is odd that this is the segment that least uses Facebook to help themselves grow even though it is the segment that can get the most out of it.

Many owners simply don't have the time to manage Facebook reliably, others do a great job. Some will hire a company like_Bourquin Group, and others will bring it in house.

One of the best I have seen to date is a Law Firm that hires an intern to do all of the posts. The partners scan the posts for a while and then the intern is pretty much on his own. Because these are normally law students, and they are sitting in a Law Firm they already have a general idea of the pain they are solving for a potential new client.

You only need to allow 15-20 minutes each week for posting and catching up with Facebook. The challenge is having the discipline to quickly scan your updates, "like" or "comment" on a few critical ones and move on to your work.

Find some compelling deal or great piece of news about your business or your industry to share. It doesn't need to be anything more than a link to another site. For instance for the business with the Racing Team, we would post the news about the new Porsche Demo Track and Facility being built in Carson California on their Facebook pages.

Keeping with the rule of solving a problem, these posts answer the problem of "Where can I go faster than 70 MPH in my Porsche?" It sounds funny but it is a real problem for people in the LA basin. Tracks are far away, and track time is expensive. Something closer to home does address a problem that is very real to many Porsche owners.

Auto fans and performance enthusiasts appreciate these links to keep them "in the know" without having to read every auto journal and website on their own. We are sort of distilling everything we heard for the week into the one or two cool tidbits for them. Our clients appreciate it and their fans and customers appreciate it.

Every business that makes money is solving a problem for people. Whether the problem is real or perceived doesn't matter. Showing them new ways to solve it or better ways that they can share with their friends is always good. Helping them understand they have a problem can get them to look closer too. That is where Facebook can be an excellent tool. Touch on a deep enough problem and everybody will "share" the solution. More importantly they will share *your* solution.

Business owners and small businesses get into trouble is trying to be all things to all people. Specialization in a niche is where you make money in small business. Proctor and Gamble, and General Electric can be more things to more people but even companies that big are not all things to all people. Small businesses must define their niche. Proctor and Gamble is just a holding center for hundreds of niche businesses better known as "brands".

The internet is already a great source of feedback and information about your business. If you try to do too many things, you'll never get any traction. If you become the best at one thing, the search engines will move your website to the number one slot. When you are in the number one slot, you keep getting the right business that makes you better and makes you more money.

Facebook works much the same way, just on a different level with a controlled audience. Because you aren't able to work around search engine rules on your Facebook page, you are much better off sticking to one niche.

Just because you select one niche to serve doesn't mean you can't serve others, it just means you market to one niche, and use the internet and Social Media to cement your number one position in that niche.

Let's use my independent Porsche repair center as an example. The primary target of our current campaign is Porsche Performance Upgrades. Beneath that we have even created a sub category for Performance Brakes, like carbon fiber.

All of that work doesn't mean that they can't do a synthetic oil change for you while you are there, or can't get a new set of tires or fix your sunroof. It just means they know they are very good at performance from their racing experience, and they can do it better than anyone else. You advertise and market the pain point you are the best at solving for your customers, and then help them with the other pains by request.

Another great example is a Salon. Many are just named after a franchise or the owners name like Kelly's Salon.

Some might go one step further and add a specialty to the name like Kelly's Hair Salon. Once you get in you might find they also do nails and offer massage therapy. The key focus is hair though.

On the internet this key focus is the keyword the entire SEO, SEM and Social Media efforts center around. IF you figure out your key focus areas and therefore your keywords, you are much more likely to reach a stronger audience and build a better business.

In larger businesses there is a subtle shift of power. The Chief Marketing Officer and Chief Information Officer are becoming one. In todays connected world the two disciplines are becoming inseparable. The customer problems and data recorded by the Information Systems can lead to the next breakthrough solution to a customer's pain. At the very least it should generate ideas for an improvement to your product or service that is very marketable.

This should be the same in your business. The person doing your Social Marketing shouldn't be a kid that has the Facebook ap on his iPhone. It needs to be an advisor that you trust, one who can give you honest feedback about what is happening to your business.

Your social media manager should understand how to use Google Analytics on your website, and Facebook analytics on your Facebook Page. They also need to know how to read that customer feedback, test it and turn it into a marketable and profitable solution.

In some cases, it might be easier for the auto shop owner to hire another mechanic or salon owner to hire another stylist and run the online marketing and social media on his or her own as they grow the business.

Multiple Location Business - As I noted earlier there are two different connections here. One is to the brand itself such as "House of Blues" or "Disney". The second is to the local fan base. Each location will grow a slightly different personality. Even McDonalds are not all exactly alike.

In addition to the local office following all of the processes for the single location business, on a corporate level there is another level. Some large restaurant chains are great at this with loyalty programs, points programs and other such memberships. The problem is, these memberships don't do anything for the customer on a local level.

Recently in Hawaii, I checked into a restaurant and posted that I lost my club card and just found out they changed the program anyway. Within minutes the manager was right there saying "Thank you for coming in". Did we get the extra appetizer, yes, did we still pay full price for the gifts that I bought, sadly yes. It didn't get me to pay the $20 for another year of the program that didn't come with a discount, but at least the local manager understood the problems with his "corporate" program and got a small up sell.

The one difficulty with Social Marketing at this juncture for Multiple Location businesses is that there is no way to have a person sign up on the local page and become a fan of the corporate page.   Instead the responsibility for reaching out to the client is the corporation's issue.

In a perfect world the corporation could post onto all of the individual locations Facebook Page with a single post for specials like Tuesday Night Reverse Happy Hour.   What I have seen done is the corporate office posts as a fan, posts individually on every page, or ask the local managers to re-post from a company page.   All of these work, none are as easy as they could be, and multiple identical posts aren't as effective.   The point of this is to solve the customers problems.   A guy in Sacramento looking for pizza may have a totally different desire than one in Boston when it is -32.

I got a great tweet from a bar a couple of years ago during a record heat wave.

"Our beer is cold, and AC is included Free. $1 off first beer with this Tweet"

That is direct and effective marketing.

VIII. Posting Techniques

Everybody gets writers block once in a while, so here are some great ways to get good content that you can post each week. At the absolute minimum, post every other week. Ideally once or twice a week is about perfect.

A post doesn't have to be long to be good, it just needs to be engaging. Many times just a link or a photo will work perfectly.

The Big Picture of Posting

Posting useless information or posting nothing more than a "buy my new widget" is the fastest way to lose fans. I have even seen paid fans jump off because there was too much "spam".

Spam used to mean only bulk email, now it refers to any message that is basically an ad posted to any format online where lots of people see it. Even a website can be considered "spammy" these days. As the writer, remember you are the host of your business, introducing it in a way where the reader relates to you. Don't get preachy.

Your Blog – If you have a blog, copy the link to an older but still relevant post, and link it with a couple of comments.

Someone Else's Blog – There are literally thousands of blogs out there by people offering solutions to problems for Do It Yourself or DIY types. These blogs can be a great source that you can offer links too. Your best customers will like the solution and pay you to do it for them.

To keep our ezines relevant, we have permission to repost from several other sites. You will be surprised how easily you can repost other peoples articles if you give them credit for them.

For instance, Randy Jackson of SunPoweredEVs.com lets us repost anything he writes as long as it links to his site. Since he isn't a competitor to any client, we use his work regularly at no charge. He gets a better reach and we get better content. Win-Win.

Online Magazines – Sites like BeachStreetNews.com have articles posted that you can link to. You can sometimes submit your own articles or buy "advertorial" articles. An "Advertorial" article is a professionally written editorial with the sole purpose of educating people about your business and product

Online Articles – Use Caution here, most people that write on places like ezinearticles.com have links to their site imbedded. Rather than use the article, look through your topic area for ideas.

IX. Advertising on Facebook

OK, I know FREE was in the title of the book *How To Market On Facebook for Free*, where this section came from, but sometimes spending a little money is a smart move. Advertising the right way on Facebook can help to accelerate your growth and test your market quicker. None of this is suggesting you spend more than $50 a month for any one goal, and this isn't really required to succeed. It just helps you go faster.

There are three basic goals with advertising on Facebook. First you can advertise with a goal of getting people to *like* your page. Second you can advertise so that people to a tab and get a sales landing page to begin a sales funnel.

Finally you can advertise for a direct sale.

These three goals almost occur in order, making a marketing plan on Facebook very straight forward.

At the beginning your page needs likes, so you advertise to people who are more likely to *like* your page. Once you have somewhere between 30 and 100 likes, you can probably move on to the second goal.

Getting those first likes help you lock up your username and gets some social linking to get your message out each time you post. Without those links, you might just end up posting to yourself.

Once you have your minimum likes, there is no need to keep paying to reach out for likes. Now it is time to move to the second goal and start working on your marketing funnel.

Here you can create a tab page that is either a landing page asking for their information as in exchange for some information that they want. Remember, this is the ethical bribe to get their email, phone number or address to get them started in your sales funnel.

Finally, you can advertise deals directly to people who have already liked your page. It is this third goal where owners rush the plan or get to aggressive and start losing likes and don't get any sales. Managing your sales funnel here is tricky, so watch your likes to gauge your aggressiveness. If your likes continue to grow and people are buying, then you are offering a deal they like. If you aren't selling and likes are declining STOP.

Advertising on Facebook can be either PPC or CPM, and so far our testing has been that CPM works best for the first goal of adding likes, and the second for leading people to a sales funnel. PPC is best saved for direct sales, and if you are getting clicks, and no sales, you know what to work on.

Keep your budgets small and pay attention daily and to postings. The market will tell you what you are doing right, what you are doing wrong and most importantly, what they want. All you have to do is listen to what you fans are telling you.

Warning!
Watch your ad budget and performance. Click Through Rates or CTR of .01% to 1.5% are very normal. This means on a CPM campaign, you will get somewhere between 10 and 150 clicks per thousand views.

Anything less than .01% you need to work on your ad or change your demographics. If you get more, then you nailed it if those numbers also become fans.

When clicks don't become fans in stage one and like your page, it means your ad doesn't take them where they thought they were going. If you set an expectation in an ad, then you better meet it.

During phase II, Your CTR should remain the same, but data collection rates can vary here from 5% to 65% depending on what they think they are getting out of the deal.

At phase III, you want click to purchase rates above 10%. These people should already be fans, and if they click at least one out of ten should by, if not, look at the ad and look at your offer, product or service. A disconnect here can get very expensive very quick.

When a new client tells me they don't want to be "tied to a pay per click campaign", they don't realize that they are always tied to some kind of marketing if they own a business. PPC if used right can be very cost effective. The trick is to test all ads, and all offers so you know what your market will pay you for. Remember, there is no free lunch, even in internet marketing.

Google+

Google+ is a new section of Google, that appears to be replacing iGoogle. One of the difficulties in dealing with Google is you never know what they are going to do next. One day they launch iGoogle, one day you get a note it is going away. They have done the same thing for several products. For now, even though Google is not a major player in social media or marketing, their overall reach in Search can't be ignored.

Google+ today is much bigger than it was a year ago, and several times bigger than it was when I built my first account. This is *NOT* going to be the answer everything guide to Google+. What this is intended to be is a focused guidebook for business owners or managers who want to get better results from their Google+ usage as it relates to business. There are going to be a few "don'ts" and a few "do's". Only the key areas that you need to work in for business are going to be covered.

If you followed the Facebook section, you will see this is very similar.

You have a business to run and a life to lead. The idea here is that Google+ is a time killer if you don't use it right and at the same time you have to be the real you or your friends will abandon you. Starting with friends is the crux of any Google+ presence.

When I work with small business owners or teach my seminars I refer to Internet Presence often. Internet Presence for a small business like the girl who bathes my two Australian Shepherd dogs might only be a Google+ Presence. She just recently got an official listing on Yelp! and is so busy even her Google+ Page is out of date.

For the context of this book, I will be focused on Google+ Presence only. If you don't have one, this will help you get started, if you do have one, I hope you will find some nuggets that you can use to make some significant improvements in the results you are getting for the time and effort you put in.

Your Google+ Profile

For a business owner who is working a small business on the side, this is the scariest place to be. Your boss and your job will eventually find out that you are moonlighting and advertising it on Google+. Now that Google+ no longer allows dual profiles, you have a decision to make.

For established business owners, or people starting a new venture who are focused on that venture, this is an easy section to cover.

The first steps of this section are the basis of your Google+ marketing program.

2015 Update Bonus- Google removed the requirement to have a Google + account and Google + profile to have your business listed on Google +. We still think it is a good idea to have these accounts as long as Google still has the sign up page

Step One: Get a Google+ Profile - If you don't have one, you need one. You can't own the Google+ Page for your business if you don't. If you don't claim your Google+ Page and prove you own it, someone else can post incorrect information. Someone once saw my client walk into her bakery at 6 am, so until we claimed the Google+ Page for her, the hours said open at 6 am. Several customers weren't happy.

Getting a Google+ Profile is easy, just go to http:// plus.google.com right on the first page is the basic sign up form and a green button that says sign up. If you do it from a computer with a couple of good pictures you can upload, that is even better.

Spend a couple of dollars and get a good profile photo.

Step Two: Build Your Profile - Your Google+ profile needs to be the real you. A little personal history is fine but not too much. I have my college, high school, and military units posted to make it easier for any of those guys to find me and get in contact with me. Again, I don't waste time on Google+ reading peoples life stories every day. I just try to build a picture of who I am as a business owner and consultant and how I can help people and businesses.

Google+ doesn't yet have the formatting and flexibility of Facebook, so keep up and make sure you keep the photos and background up to date.

My personal profile timeline shows me at different marketing events. My photo rarely changes and shows me outside doing something. The intent is to create a mental picture that I am outside and marketing for my clients all the time. Spend a little time thinking about your profile picture and cover photo and how they can help visually support your brand both personally and professionally.

As you build your profile always keep in mind three things, your brand, your business and your customer. If you aren't in the outdoor recreation business, don't post a hundred pictures of you and your family camping. Maybe just one to let people know you are real.

Customers are ruthless, they don't want to visit your store or office to find you out goofing off, they want to know you are always working to make their life better and solve their problems. Don't brag about how much time you don't work on Google+. Even though the profile is private to the people you approve as friends, they can share it with their friends and it will come back to you like bad online karma. Perception is everything.

Never Consider Anything On Google+ As "Private".

Now that you have built your Google+ profile, here are some tips on how to use it.

1. Check in with your smart phone at every business that you can where you know the owner and are friendly with them. Ask them to do the same.

2. "Follow" all of those same businesses and ask them to do the same.

Google+ has some good apps for doing this right from your smart phone.

Step Three: Build a Page - This one is a little tougher. Your page is your website on Google+ and it might be the first and last impression of your business that people see so make it count. The worst part is that you might already have a Google+ page and not know it.
If you have a physical location and a phone number it is very likely you have a Google Places Page already. You should be able to claim the page and connect it to your page. If someone else claimed your page, you may have to jump through some hoops to get it back.

This is where you have to remember you aren't paying Google+ $19.95 a month for web hosting. So far all of this is free so it might take time if you run into problems with pages or people creating fake pages.

My staff is all around the world so when we build Google+ pages and need to verify information it is a little more work than if you do it yourself I am sure.

If your business has five locations, build a separate page for each location.

The first step to building a page is to search for your business and see if anyone else has built one. Just type the name of your business in the search box while you are logged in. If there is already a page or a place that is your business, click on it.

If you find a Google+ Page for your business that you don't own, then you will need to contact Google. Unlike Google places where you can simply "claim the page" by clicking a button, you will need to prove it is your business.

If there isn't a page already for your business or a place for your business, simply click on the "more" or three dots on the left side of the menu. Sometimes there is a "create page" button on the right of the page. If not click the menu and the square symbol for creating a page.

Fill out as much information in the Basic Information Section as possible. While you are in that section click each of the menu options on the left panel to get as much information online as possible.

The more of this you get up now, the more likely you are to get Followers that stick.

Double check all of the simple things, like your address, phone number and hours. You would be amazed at how many people overlook that stuff.

Step Five: Get Followed - This is where you might spend a little money for the first time. Google doesn't have names like Facebook, so this is where the two online efforts become different.

With Google, you can get a pay per click ad to send people to your page, just like you do for your website. This is a very difficult task because you are direct marketing a soft sell. On Facebook, they profile members so they can target "interested" people for you.

If you have a physical store, a QR code or small sign asking people to check in or like your page may be the best methods to add followers.

Another method of getting follows is the ethical bribe. Give a discount or deal to the first 100 people who like you and come in the shop. If you have a busy store, 30 likes won't take long at all. If you are an Internet Marketing Company where clients never visit your office, this method may not work.

Finally you I am sure that soon you will be able to "buy" follows. Just go to eBay and search "Google+ follows", "Facebook likes" or "twitter fans".   I don't personally ascribe to this method for small businesses, but it does add numbers which some people feel they need.

For very small or very targeted niche, I don't like the idea of buying big numbers of fans because your real fans might take a look and see that your little shop of magic in Tempe Arizona has 800 fans in the Philippines and you don't sell online. Being fake won't fly for long in social media. If you choose to go this route, make sure you go full speed to add real followers so you have some real people.

Step Six: Post - This is the step that causes the most confusion and frustration across the board with business owners, consultants and celebrities. If they turn over the responsibility too early, or without enough direction, the posts get out of hand and occasionally can offend people.

The photos and information on your Google+ Page should be geared around two areas. Photos and information about your staff will help your influencers feel "connected" to them. If someone has a baby and they are ok sharing it, share it.

The other area is about solving problems for your customers. Every business solves problems for customers and nothing else. Even the Chef at Cake Tahoe is solving the problem of the perfect cake for the perfect wedding, or the problem of what treat to give a child after an accomplishment or even a different kind of birthday party with cupcakes so some can have chocolate and others get vanilla.

Every time you post, are you connecting or problem solving? You should be, so if you aren't doing either, don't post. If you can't come up with at least one connection or problem solution each week, you need to slow down and listen to your customers; they have problems that will build your business.   Trust me when I say, your business problems won't build your business.

If you delegate your social media posting and your Social Marketing, make sure that the person or service you delegate to understands you, your purpose and direction, your business and your customer.   Google+ is a tool for you to connect to your customer via your business. Never violate that trust and be very careful not to sever that connection unintentionally.

Posting is the place where each business gets a little different in how I advise people to post or to create TABS. So for this step and the next step, I will include some examples based on the size of the business.   These are the last steps on your roadmap to success in Social Media as long as you stay honest with your fans and give them something worth sharing, you will see a difference in your business and you won't need to live online.

Yelp!

Yelp! is probably the biggest in entertainment and dining among the "local directories" that have a social aspect. The competition in this section of social media is fierce and can get expensive. If you are in the hospitality business in any way, you need to keep up with Yelp!. You don't need to necessarily buy advertising, or deals, but you can't afford to let your reviews go unanswered, or your information get out of date on Yelp!

To get started you first need to become a "Yelper", which is a member of Yelp!. You will build a personal profile, and I suggest using it to checkin at several places you like to build credibility, and solidify your account.

Next you will need to claim your business, or build a page for one. To do that though you have to go to Yelp! for business owners. It is a totally different section. In the business owners area you can claim your business and edit all of the information about it.

Foursquare

Foursquare is the even more social version of the big "local directories" when it comes to the hospitality business. Very much like Yelp! in the ability to search and find places to go, Foursquare adds a heavy emphasis on where your "friends" are.

While similar to Yelp!, claiming your business and updating the information isn't as difficult. Getting a Foursquare account and posting a few reviews won't hurt either.

Manta

Manta is primarily a business to business local directory however we have seen some very profitable and unexpected cross pollination with our clients on Manta. If you service businesses in any way, Manta can be a great low cost solution. For under $40 a month you can get a premium listing which removes your competitors ads.

For instance, a pizza place might get catering calls from local businesses. A business owner looking for a copy machine repair company might just get bored and research "carbon fiber brakes" for his sports car.

The ads on Manta should be tested on a case by case basis. We have had very mixed luck with buying actual ads on Manta. As an agency, Manta isn't as easy to work with as other sites. As of this writing, each business can only have one listing. If you have multiple locations, you will need to create multiple accounts. When you put multiple locations under a single listing, you get some very funny data from Manta. For instance we got a weekly report showing a pizza place had 5 views for SEO, an auto repair center was viewed 32 times for pizza, and our business had 45 views for auto brakes.

Fortunately, we test all of our posts and we know the right names and services are showing up together and I am sure that at some point this minor issue will get fixed. For now if you have multiple locations, set up multiple users.

Manta is quite simple to set up. If your business has a landline type telephone number or has a business license more than a few months old, it is likely that you have a business page already on Manta. All you have to do is create and account and claim the page.

If you buy the premium listing, check your website analytics after about four months. If you aren't getting good response or any direct business from Manta viewers, cancel the premium listing.

Test and monitor all the marketing you do online so you do don't spend any money that doesn't bring in more money.

MySpace

MySpace is the one major site we have nearly overlooked. For the most part the user demographics don't fit our clients. Since it was acquired by Justin Timberlake and his investment group, MySpace has seen a turn around and is now a social site to pay attention too.

If your business is in the entertainment business, MySpace might be your first step.

Follow the same rules as Facebook or Google + when it comes to posts and seeking fans. MySpace will let you set up a single profile as a business, and due to the very focused support of the entertainment and music industry, MySpace is a different type of site.

Having a profile on MySpace is free, and so it is a good idea to have one.

LinkedIn

LinkedIn is a very different player in this space and as such requires a different approach.   Businesses can advertise, but don't necessarily have or need a profile or page. The real idea behind LinkedIn, is to keep business people connected in a dedicated environment.   Where Facebook Posts are 80-90% personal or entertainment, LinkedIn is generally business networking and the posts are related to specific industries and groups.

If you run a business service company like I do, then you should have a profile on LinkedIn and you should make it public.   This helps with linking, SEO and getting more overall exposure online at no additional cost.

If you are inclined you can join groups to ask and answer questions related to your field. What I have found is that about 50% of the posts are people tooting their own horn, so there isn't as much learning and education as there could be.

That said, LinkedIn should be treated like a Social Media site. If you aren't careful you can get sucked in only to look up and notice you are the only one in the office. Use it carefully and wisely. For owners, your profile is your business profile, aka a free ad.

LBLO - Local Business Listing Optimization. A system that automatically updates as many as 50 local directories at once. This keeps changes to the business simple.   If you don't have time to manage it, you still need to make monthly updates and follow up. The LBLO is mostly an automated system and if anything doesn't match it doesn't work.

At FireRock.Online we offer self service local business listing optimization and full service local business listing optimization services. The key difference being how much time you have to spend each month to make sure you're coupons and bonuses are kept up-to-date.

If you don't keep your local listing bonuses up to date then it might be money wasted.

X. Hire Good Contractors (cheap)

Hiring out the work for your business can be a very expensive proposition if done wrong. My company rebuilds at least one website every quarter that a company spent good money on. One of my coaches is always talking about improving the quality of our websites.

This is where most owners get into trouble. They pay up front for a fancy website with graphics and custom images. Six months later they are calling my office because the website is still 11,889 out of 19,525 on Google for their business category. Before we can work on getting the search rankings up, we usually replace the website.

What we mean about improving the quality of a website is the usability and readability of the site. The overall appearance should be clean and relatively simple, and now very mobile friendly.

If you have more time than money right now, there are lots of experienced contractors on upwork.com (formerly odesk.com) or elance.com who can build you a great website for a fraction of what it costs to get one built through an agency.

Our rates at our Website Hosting business, FireRock.Online are among the lowest I know of, and for some businesses that still may not be in the budget.

Hiring overseas talent to work for your business, or any online contract talent isn't hard. The most important thing is to know exactly what you want. If you don't know, then you need an agency or a coach to help guide you. That is why we offer online training with monthly coaching.

If you want my help it will cost you several hundred dollars an hour. Instead you can get training that breaks all of this information into monthly actionable steps and has a conference call you can ask questions and have your Internet Presence program reviewed by us. All of this for a year is less than a couple of hours of consulting time.

Before you hire any contract staff, I suggest you write down an outline like this:

Project Webfix:

I want-
-Easy to Use Website. Wordpress maybe?
-To be able to update site myself
-To be able to control access to the site.
-To link to my youTube videos
-To link my Podcast
-Mobile ready version to catch customers on the go.
-Email List Capture - three lists, one for each Target.
-To Target

> **a**. People who are looking for a better job (teach them how to find their niche and market themselves better)
>
> **b**. Small business owners who want to create their own Internet Presence campaign (teach them how to find their niche and market their business better)
>
> **c**. Small business owners who want to grow their business to the next level (teach them how to grow their niche and market their business better)

-Member ship site - secure, paid monthly or annually

I don't want-
-Flash video that won't play on iPad or iPhone
-More than three main pages - Keep it focused
-People who aren't serious, no tire kickers
-More than three mouse clicks to watch a video or get to a buy now page.

My Contractor should:
-Respond to changes within 1 business day
-Be able to make changes in 2 business days
-Outside of US ok
-Fluent in US English

I like the following sites:

www.socalbeachrealtor.com easy to read
www.caketahoe.com – Great photos

My site should look like these a little.

With this simple list in hand you can now go post to odesk.com or elance.com and request proposals. You will get tons of "canned" responses like.

Dear Bourquin Group,
I find that I am very capable of taking care of your project.
Please hire me and I will do it.
Regards
Joe Brown

Just ignore all of those types of emails. Many are from agencies and unqualified people. Personally I prefer to search for people and send them a message directly.

Avoid Spam, Hire Direct.

You do this by making your job proposal "private". Then you can search for contractors using your criteria like "Wordpress" and "English Speaking". More than once I have been surprised and found way over qualified women who chose to stay home after having a baby who are both US and Canadian for just a couple of dollars more than someone overseas.

Many of my coaches use elance.com. For whatever reason, I mostly use odesk.com. Probably because I have several teams built there and some of my contractors have been with me for more than three years now. I also have a back office staff in Manila, but they can't do everything, so I make sure my oDesk.com teams are ready to go.

If you want more help, we have a members only site that includes monthly live coaching calls and followup to help you stay on track with your one thing.

Visit elite.bourquingroup.com if you want to learn more.

XI. The 2015 Bonus Chapter

Since the first book has come out we have launched a new Website Hosting Business and learned a lot about how businesses start-up and how they miss the mark.

There are two areas to consider about your business before you move forward. Normally I only share this with my clients, but I decided to make it a bonus chapter because it is too important for you to miss.

When I work with a client, I put their business into one of three categories;
1. A "One Shot" or "Emergency" Business.
2. A Impulse Business
3. A Relationship Business

My goal is try and move every client I work with as close to a relationship business as possible. There are some where that just isn't practical. Auto accident attorneys are only needed after you get an accident.

These are different than an impulse business like a donut shop that has a great location and no need to advertise.

Plumbing is one of the most common outside cover advertisements you see on the yellow pages along with accident attorneys. Generally speaking both of these businesses are one shot or emergency businesses. I hope you don't need a personal accident attorney more than once in your life, ideally you won't need one ever.

Plumbing is slightly different because you might just want to add a sink moving it closer to an impulse business. Unless of course they have maintained relationship with you from the time that they made the last emergency call. So where does this all lead?

The first question you must ask yourself before spending a penny on marketing is "What kind of business do I have and how will I position it?".

What I mean by this question is how are you going to compete. And more importantly how are you going to engage your clients. Ideally you want to find away to move your business into the category of a relationship business. You will spend less money on marketing and have more profitable customers an emergency or impulse business..

When most businesses start out, they make the mistake of thinking they are an emergency business. The funny thing is very few businesses fall under this category.

Personal injury attorneys, hospitals, and plumbers fall under this category. These are businesses that you don't know you need until you need them. When your toilet is overflowing at 2 o'clock in the morning you need an emergency plumber.

Keep in mind an emergency plumber can also be a regular plumber and a construction plumber. If they market correctly they will use the business of the emergency plumber to lead customers into a relationship. Almost any business can do this.

A new construction plumber who builds a relationship business with a builder or several builders is different from and marketed differently then an emergency plumber. They also have significantly different fee schedules.

An emergency plumber charges a very large "convenience fee". They have to do this in order to keep someone on call 24 hours a day seven days a week and pay for those ridiculously expensive yellow pages front page ads.

When most people start a brand-new business they buy advertising as if it is an emergency they need customers. The problem is if they own a pizza restaurant, a cupcake store or even an auto shop, most people won't have an emergency that causes them to need pizza, a cupcake or an oil change.

We try to teach all of our clients to key things:

First is that customers need escalating value or they get bored. You have to offer them something more every time they come in. They might not buy it for several months but they need to know it's there to give them a reason to come back.

For instance in our website hosting business, We start off with a loss leader. We give away a free report in exchange for the customer's email address. That gets them on our mailing list. In a world of online marketing this is called the"ethical bribe".

Once there on that mailing list, they receive a series of email messages asking them to get a copy of my latest book and all they have to do is pay shipping and handling. So even at step two we are still losing a little bit of money on every new customer obtained.

Once they have the book in their hand, We move them into the profit categories and try to sell them very inexpensive website hosting or local listing services. From there we can increase the value of our services by adding online advertising management, Professional copywriting and consulting services.

The end goal is to get them into one of our business management courses which is totally unrelated to our website hosting business. The whole idea is to give them more value every time we engage them.

This keeps us out of the high dollar "Emergency advertising" like plumbers, Tow truck drivers and truck accident attorneys have to pay for.

This leads to the second key which is relationship marketing. When you have a line of products that increase in value as the increasing price and profitability, you create a relationship business.

Now you can't do any of this until you understand the why of your business. We are little kids we're always asking why. As adults we think we stop asking why but the reality is every time someone walks into a business we ask ourselves "Why is this business here and what can it do for me?"

The exact same thing happens online when they hit your website. If you can't answer why you're there in a few simple words then that is an area we would focus on.

Appendix I - SEO Copy Writing Example

Keyword Phrase "Water Heater Replacement"

Copy Before:

Welcome to Johns Plumbing. We have been serving the local area for nearly 15 years. At Johns Plumbing, we offer complete services such as drain cleaning and clearing, root removal, faucet replacement and water heater installation.

At Johns plumbing we offer the latest in water and energy saving technology such as low flow and two button toilets. Whatever your plumbing needs, Johns Plumbing is here to serve.

Copy After:

Water Heater Replacements are something we all need to deal with. If your Water Heater is gurgling, or you aren't getting hot water any more, it might be time to get it checked. If your water heater is more than 15 years old, or if you live in an area with hard water, those noises might be a sign that it is time for a Water Heater Replacement.

If you want to save energy when it comes time for a Water Heater Replacement, consider tankless. A tankless water heater can save up to 15% for a normal household. You might save more with a tankless water heater if you travel or are away from home for extended periods.

Notice the difference? Only one service, water heater replacement is mentioned and only one option, tankless. The keyword appears more than once and parts of the keyword are used throughout creating more connections for the search engines to use.

Many business owners will respond with "But we do all of the other stuff!" As a consultant first, marketing agency second, we have to stick to the program that works. Get really good at one thing and the rest is gravy. If you are number one in water heater replacements, you might have so much work you don't have time to clear drains. Less gear on the truck and faster installations because of the practice lead to higher profits without adding people. It is that simple. We have seen it in every business we work with.

The search engines reward highly focused and effective businesses and so do customers.

Appendix II -Bonus Rules for Print Media.

Here is the toughest lesson for all small business owners to wrap their heads around. Specialization pays period.

Just like your Internet Presence campaign, any print ads should say the three keywords with one look.

Think about the last time you saw a plumbers van driving down the road. Do You remember anything about it? Do you remember enough to call them if your sink clogged right now?

The smart companies have a simple name, a simple solution and a easy to remember visual on the side.

The newbies, desperate for work have a list like this:
Drain cleaning, water heater repair, new plumbing, remodels, gas lines, leak finding, galvanized pipe replacement, PTFE pipe systems.

All of that is in a little font that nobody can read or remember when they pass the truck on the way to work.

These guys do the same thing in their print ads.

The smart guys have the same logo and a picture of the van. The ad will have just one service on it like "Water Heater Replacement".

If you think of your entire business and can target 10 keywords or less, your online marketing will be more successful.

Remember a "keyword" is used interchangeably with "keyword phrase".

If you can use 5 keywords or less for print marketing, and ideally, just target one key word like "Water Heater Replacement" your print media ads will do much better.

Don't overwhelm and confuse people telling them everything you CAN do. Tell them about the ONE thing you do better than anyone else. If you don't have one thing, figure it out and market it.

As a business consultant this is the first task I help business owners with. When you do one thing very well, it is easier to hire and train your staff, you get faster and better at it, and most importantly. Out become very profitable at it.

When I owned my two home theater stores, I didn't take this lesson to heart. I watched in envy as two of my competitors did, and at the time I didn't get it. One only sold a specific brand of universal remote. His guys were so good we subcontracted out our jobs to them. Many times he was making more on the remote and programming than I was making on the TV, Receiver, Speakers and installation, and my stores even sold the remote!

The other guy only sold one brand of TV, and one system. The complete package left his shop preprogrammed. He also had a better bottom line with less overhead than I had.

Eventually I did figure out this rule, and dropped 60% of the brands we carried. Whenever a customer asked for a different brand we would simply explain that it is better that we know a few products cold than be familiar with a lot of products.

Sales remained flat, overhead and purchasing dropped, returns dropped, call backs dropped. So on the same sales profits were several times better. A year later we saw sales growth and kept the same (higher) margins.

I am sharing this with you because I don't want you to struggle trying to do everything. I've tried and dozens of business owners that I have worked with have tried. To date I haven't met one that didn't do better by doing their one thing.

The mission of my books, business and articles is to help you move towards your destination by helping you find and become great at your "one thing". Part of this is helping people avoid the big mistake I made and find their one thing.

When you break the code on this little secret of business, Focus on your "one thing", you'll be able to quickly evaluate everything you do in your business and marketing. You just have to ask "Does this say we do our *one thing*". If not, send it back.

175

Scott Bourquin is a Decorated Combat pilot/former Air Force pilot-turned Commercial Pilot-amateur Racing Car Driver and Actor.

During his military service, Scott served in several capacities beginning as a Security Police Team Member and retiring 20 years later from the Air Force Reserves as a Air Force Reserve KC-10 Instructor Pilot and Chief of Information Systems.

Scott flew several tours in support of Operations Enduring Freedom and Iraqi Freedom and was "name selected" to represent the Air Force Reserves at the 100th Anniversary of Flight Celebration at EAA AirVenture Oshkosh. When not flying in the Reserves, Scott was flying as Commercial Pilot for American Airlines, and building several businesses.

Scott has made his share of mistakes too.

Missing out on an F-16 flying slot and building a business that completely wiped out the gains from two previous businesses are among the more notable missteps in Scott's life.

It is through these mistakes that Scott was able to understand personally why we succeed and why we fail. He has taken that understanding to create personal and business coaching programs that help people and businesses find their "one thing" so they don't have to experience any more failures, and understand why they haven't reached the level of success they deserve.

As the Chief Focus Coach/CEO of Bourquin Group since its inception in 2009, Scott now combines calculated precision required in the cockpit to *"Getting new businesses, new brands, new products, to fly...".* He offers Business Performance & consultancy services and online coaching programs.

Scott wants to share his methods of success with you, so you too can live the life you deserve without the frustrations and failures he had to endure.

Scott holds a degree in Business–Information Resource Management from San José State University. He also has gained hands-on insight into industry best practices in leadership and innovation from his former employers, to include the likes of Apple, Airtouch (Now Verizon-Vodaphone) and Stanford University.

An Internet Marketing Authority, Best Selling Author© & Keynote Speaker, Scott has delivered presentations and live training to small companies and national conventions.

Contact the <u>Bourquin Group</u> to learn more about online or live training for your business.

Other Books by Scott Bourquin

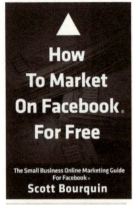

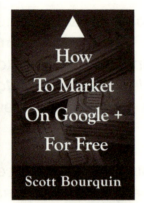

Other books featuring Scott Bourquin

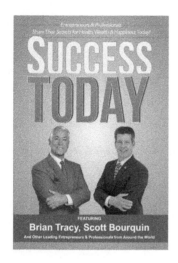